**Complete Guide
to the
Fifty Defenses in Football**

Complete Guide
to the
Fifty Defenses in Football

Jack Olcott

Parker Publishing Company, Inc.
West Nyack, N.Y.

© 1976, *by*

PARKER PUBLISHING COMPANY, INC.

West Nyack, N.Y.

Library of Congress Cataloging in Publication Data

Olcott, Jack.
   Complete guide to the fifty defenses in football.

   Includes index.
   1. Football--Defense. I. Title.
GV951.18.O42   796.33'22   76-14403
ISBN 0-13-160390-6

Printed in the United States of America

Dedicated to my wife, Suzi.

Other books by the author:

Football Coach's Guide to Successful Pass Defense
Football's Fabulous Forty Defense
Complete Book of Triple Option Football

How This Book Will Help You Win

The modern Fifty Defense with its split ends, flankers, twins, and slot adjustments is the most popular and the strongest defense in high school and college football today. It has permeated the professional football ranks, with most professional teams having adopted the "Fifty-Look" into their defensive package.

In this book are detailed the most complete and up-to-date adjustments, assignments, and techniques of the Fifty Defenses to help stop any offensive attack. The author describes and illustrates the best methods of adjusting the Fifty Defenses to stop the opponent's favorite running and passing plays.

This book is a coach's Bible of how to stop the top running plays from the various Triple Option maneuvers to the most successful "I's," cut, or sprint draw play. Chapters 10 and 11 describe and illustrate the secondary play to stop the most successful passing attack from the short check-up passes to the bomb.

Written in such a manner that the coach may want to give a copy to each of his staff members or to pass the book along to each player on the defense, this defensive book is a simple, basic and logically sound coach's guide.

The author believes that execution is critical to winning. Consistent success in execution is predicated upon the proper coaching of football techniques, and here the reader will find the most up-to-date coaching techniques currently being used by most successful football coaches.

This book is of great value not only for the defensive coaching staff, but also for offensive coaches in helping them recognize the defensive alignments, formations, and techniques for which they have to prepare.

The text tells how to make on-the-field key defensive adjustments to stop the opponent's offense in clutch game situations.

Illustrated here is a complete guide of how to coach the Fifty Defense. This guide is not limited to the Oklahoma Defense, but includes all facets of the Monster, Bubble, Revert, Fifty-three, and Stack defenses. The various aspects of the three- and four-deep secondary coverage techniques and assignments are also covered.

The Fifty Defenses have been systematically organized and illustrated, so these techniques and coaching points may be adapted to any defense on either the high school or college level.

Many of the defensive principles and ideas found in the Fifty multi-defensive concept may give even the most experienced coach a unique insight into a specific phase of defensive football.

To stop a potent offensive attack decisively, the defensive coach must understand the intricate details of his complete defensive package. That is what this book is all about. Each phase of the Fifty Defense is explained and illustrated. The various adjustments, stunts, and key coaching points are described in detail. All of these defensive ideas and principles can be easily applied to any defensive alignment the reader may select.

This text teaches the coach how to out-execute his opponent. There is an emphasis on how to successfully coach defensive techniques. The coach no longer must use the old adage, "Just play football," when asked how to defeat a scramble block, take on an inside-out trap, or feather the pitch-keep option.

The author describes and illustrates how you may include the whole or segments of each chapter into your team's playbook for each of your defensive football players, and kicks off each chapter with a concise description and explanation of each defense, packaged in one comprehensive chart.

The stems, stunts, and defensive blitzes are explained in step-by-step sequences. This book describes the flexibility of the "Fifty's" adjustments, shifts, short-yardage blitzes, victory defenses, and pass defensive assignments, all combined under a unique defensive numbering system. The contents in this text will help you better prepare and teach defensive football fundamentals in practice sessions and will make you a more strategically oriented coach during the game.

Jack Olcott

Table of Contents

3.   The Stunting Fifty Defense *(cont.)*

4.   Fifty Monster Slant Defense . . .63

7.   The Fifty Bubble and Revert Stunting Defenses *(cont.)*

8.   How to Coach the Fifty-three Pro Defense   .   .   .125

9.   Teaching the Fifty-three Stack Defense   .   .   .149

10.   The Three-Deep Pass Defense   .   .   .161

10. The Three-Deep Pass Defense *(cont.)*

11. The Four-Deep Pass Defense . . . **195**

11.   The Four-Deep Pass Defense *(cont.)*

**Complete Guide
to the
Fifty Defenses in Football**

1

Introducing the Fifty Oklahoma Defense

The Fifty Oklahoma Defense, known throughout the football world as the 5-4 Oklahoma Defense, has stood the test of time. Through the years, coaches have added adjustments, stunts, and successful blitzes to the Fifty Oklahoma Defense, but the basic Fifty Defense is still being used in winning fashion versus the modern offensive cycles, including the Veer I and Wishbone Triple Option teams.

This is it—the Basic Fifty Defense—the nuts and bolts. The successful coach must master these fundamentals, details, and coaching points before he goes on to succeeding chapters on the Fifty Slant, Fifty Monster, Fifty-one, Fifty-three Stack, Fifty Loop, Fifty Blitzes, and the many other Fifty Defenses and Fifty adjustments.

HOW TO NUMBER THE DEFENDERS

I have modernized the defensive numbering system so that we can assign a defender over, inside, outside, or in the gap all along the line of scrimmage. Utilizing this unique numbering system, all of the defenders along the defensive front are numbered. This simplified numbering system gives each defender not only his alignment, but also his defensive technique assignment.

The reason I used this complete numbering system is to cut down on lengthy alignment explanations in staff and player-coaches' meetings. When the coach says, "Play an '0' technique," the defender is given his exact alignment, stance, and technique to use against all forms of blocking patterns. He knows that an "0" technique tells him to line nose-up on the offensive center. He is given his offensive key, whom he is to read once the ball has been put into play, and the technique he will use against all the various blocking patterns he will face throughout the season.

Our numbering system starts from the center and works out from either side. A head-up or nose-up position on an offensive lineman is an even number. All gaps from the center out are odd numbers (Diagram 1-1). If the defender lines up on the line of scrimmage, shading the inside

DIAGRAM 1-1

or outside shoulder of an offensive linemen, we use two numbers for this defender. The first number is the nearest even number and the second number is the nearest gap ("21," "45," etc.; see Diagram 1-2).

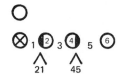

DIAGRAM 1-2

NUMBERING THE FIFTY DEFENSE

The middle guard lines up on the nose of the offensive center in an "0" alignment (Diagram 1-3).

Since the linebackers line up off the line of scrimmage, the first digit is paired. Thus, the defender who lines up two to three yards off the line of scrimmage will have two or three digits. The Fifty linebacker lines up

DIAGRAM 1-3   **DIAGRAM 1-4**

on the outside shoulder of the offensive guard, off the line of scrimmage; therefore, the defender's first digit is paired and he is assigned a "223" alignment (Diagram 1-4). Defensive tackles and defensive ends also shade the outside of their respective assigned offensive linemen in their "45" and "67" alignments (Diagram 1-5).

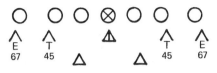

DIAGRAM 1-5

If the Fifty Defense adjusts into a knockdown alignment to the split end's side, the Fifty Knockdown adjustment would look like Diagram 1-6.

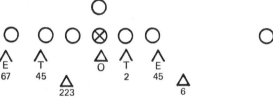

DIAGRAM 1-6

Here is an illustration of some of the various Fifty Defenses discussed in this book. Our Fifty-three Pro Defense aligns and is numbered as pictured in Diagram 1-7. The Fifty Bubble Defense lines up as featured

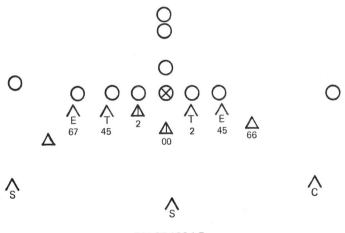

DIAGRAM 1-7

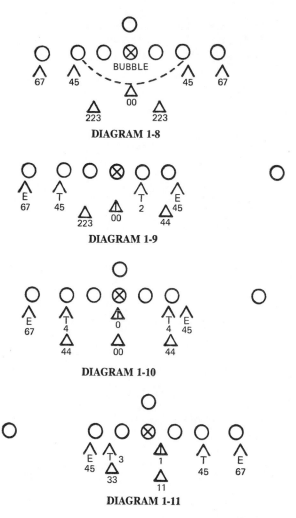

DIAGRAM 1-8

DIAGRAM 1-9

DIAGRAM 1-10

DIAGRAM 1-11

in Diagram 1-8. The Fifty Revert Defense is illustrated in Diagram 1-9, while the Fifty-three Stack Defense is aligned and numbered as featured in Diagram 1-10. The Fifty Gap Stack Defense would look like Diagram 1-11.

WHY THE FIFTY DEFENSE

In the past 25 years, the offense has gone through a number of offensive cycles from the Split T, Belly T, Wing T, Power I, Pro I, Slot I,

Pro, Triple Option attacks, etc. Throughout these offensive cycles, the most popular Fifty Defense has withstood the test of time.

This Fifty Odd Defense is easily adjustable to any and all formations and is a sound balanced defense versus the offensive unit's running and passing attack. This odd nine-man front is also an excellent defense to stunt and blitz from and may be easily converted to a goal line or short-yardage defense. Thus, the Fifty Defense has it all as a sound basic defense, which minimizes extemporaneous individual techniques and eliminates individual defensive guesswork. The Fifty Defensive package is a solidly organized and planned system featuring TEAM, played with a capital "T."

FIFTY DEFENSE CONTROL

The defensive ends and tackles line up shading the offensive players' outside shoulders and use their inside flippers to control the opposition's offense. The depth of these four defenders depends upon whether we are employing a reading or attacking defense. When reading, our defenders utilize more depth; when attacking, our defenders crowd the line of scrimmage. The defensive linebackers also line up on their designated offensive players' outside and use their inside arm to control these defenders. Their depth is two to two and one-half yards off the ball. The

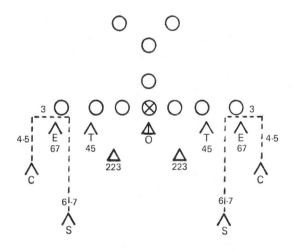

DIAGRAM 1-12

middle guard lines up on the center's nose and must control the offensive pivot man's head.

The secondary lines up approximately six to seven yards deep with the cornerbacks about three yards outside the widest receiver and four to five yards deep. The safetyman lines up approximately in the gap between the offensive tackle and tight end (Diagram 1-12).

The defensive support comes from an outside-in angle, and only the middle guard has a head-up two-gap area to defend. The defensive secondary also attacks the run from their outside-in angle. Thus, all of our defenders have the responsibility to cover their respective gap areas and turn the play back inside toward the defensive pursuit patterns.

THE FIFTY FORCING AND CONTAINING UNITS

The Fifty Defense is made up basically of two units: the forcing unit and the containing unit. The forcing unit is normally composed of the defensive ends, tackles, linebackers, and middle guard. The containing unit is generally made up of the two defensive safeties and cornerbacks. Any change in the forcing unit is made by the weakside linebacker, and any change in the containing unit is made by the weakside safetyman.

HOW TO IMPROVE THE FIFTY PURSUIT TEMPO

Outstanding team pursuit is what good basic defense is all about. To improve the Fifty team pursuit patterns, we run a lot of quick pursuit thud sessions. This means we make all of the defenders tag or bump the ball carrier. Tackling is against the rules, and the ball carrier keeps running and does not stop until the defensive coordinator blows the whistle when the last member of the defensive eleven tags the ball carrier.

During the Fifty Drill, our coaches emphasize the correct pursuit channels, making sure no defender follows the same color on the same pursuit angle. This is an all-out pursuit drill, and our players had better be sprinting one hundred percent or each individual defender will hear about it right on the spot and again at the end of practice at night school sessions.

FIFTY DEFENSE FLEXIBILITY

The Fifty Odd Defense is sufficiently flexible to stop any offensive formation we have ever seen. If the defensive players know what offensive maneuvers to expect and are able to execute their correct defensive techniques, any defensive team may be assured of a successful defensive season.

FIFTY DEFENSE EXECUTION

Execution is what defense is all about. We teach each of our defenders the strong and weak aspects of all of our defensive Fifty sets. Therefore, we build a fundamentally sound Fifty Defense and drill constant repetitions of offensive maneuvers against all of the points along the defense. Once the basic Fifty Defense is consistently sound, we add various stunts, blitzes, and adjustments to help strengthen this odd nine-man defensive front.

EXPLANATION OF THE FIFTY DEFENSIVE RESPONSIBILITY CHART

The Fifty Defensive Responsibility Chart (Diagram 1-13a) is a one-page view of the Fifty's defensive alignments, keys by progression, re-

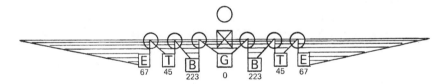

FIFTY DEFENSE RESPONSIBILITY CHART

	ALIGNMENT	KEYS BY PROGRESSION	RESPONSIBILITIES
ENDS	67	(1) End (2) Near Back (3) Fullback	End to sidelines
TACKLES	45	(1) Tackle (2) End (3) Near Back	Tackle to nose of end
LINEBACKERS	223	(1) Guard (2) Near Back (3) Fullback	Nose of Guard to nose of tackle
MIDDLE GUARD	0	(1) Center (2) Guards (3) Quarterback-Fullback	Nose of Left Guard to nose of Right Guard

DIAGRAM 1-13a

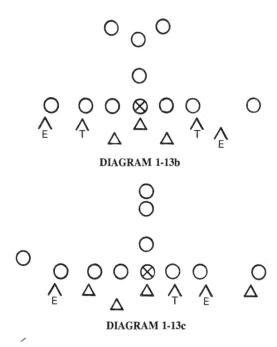

DIAGRAM 1-13b

DIAGRAM 1-13c

sponsibilities, and techniques. All of these featured coaching points are explained in concise terms and illustrated in diagrams of the Fifty's versus different offensive formations (Diagrams 1-13b and 1-13c). This gives the reader the overall picture of the assignments and responsibilities of all the defenders along the seven-man forcing unit (Diagram 1-13a).

This chart is an excellent outline for a player's defensive notebook, in which he can continually review his defensive alignments and responsibilities prior to receiving his fundamental and technical coaching points from his coaches via chalk talks, verbal quizzes, and demonstrations on the practice field.

2

Illustrated Fifty Defensive Techniques

All of the alignments, assignments, keys, reads, techniques, and fundamental defensive coaching points concerning the Fifty Defense were covered in Chapter 1 (Diagram 1-13). The following teaching aspects of the Fifty Defense have been organized, outlined by defensive position dealing with each defender's alignment and depth, stance, key, responsibility, charge, pursuit, and, most important, the execution of the proper defensive techniques to get rid of the blocker and make the tackle. All of these techniques are explained in detail and amply illustrated throughout the chapter in various descriptive diagrams.

THE MIDDLE GUARD'S "0" ASSIGNMENTS

The middle guard must be a unique type of defender—one who has the power to fight through the double team block and the quickness of a linebacker to react to the center's head and make tackles all along the defensive front.

At times this middle guard is assigned a linebacker's "00" alignment and plays this quick middle linebacker position when the Fifty Defense lines up in a Fifty Bubble or Fifty Revert position. At other times the middle guard lines up as a "2" defender (on the head of the offensive guard) whenever the Fifty-one Defense is called.

Therefore, the middle guard must be quick, agile, and powerful. He must also be able to defend from a two-point or four-point defensive stance. Continual one-on-one defensive drills are necessary to perfect the middle guard's ability to play the head of the center and control the line of scrimmage from offensive guard to guard.

"0" Alignment and Depth: The defensive middle guard is coached to line up nose-up on the offensive center. The depth is normally two feet off the ball, but the defender may wish to tighten up on the center in short-yardage plays. Depending upon the middle guard's stunt, the defender may alternate his depth from tight on the center's nose to looser off the line of scrimmage (Diagram 2-1).

DIAGRAM 2-1

Middle Guard's Line Stance: Normally we teach our new middle guard candidates to line up in a regular four-point stance. Once the "0" defender has practiced his fundamentals from this stance, he is able to use a three-point stance, if he can convince the defensive line coach he can perform more consistently from this stance.

The middle guard is coached to put less weight on his hands than do the defensive tackles. The reason for this is that the defender must reach to either his right or his left, depending upon the block of the center. Most of the middle guard's weight is distributed to his legs, while his butt is dropped lower to keep his head up. This enables the defender to react more quickly to the center's block.

Key: The "0" defender is coached to key the head and shoulders of the center. Once the ball has been snapped, the middle guard is coached to read both the center and guard's block.

Responsibilities: If crowding the center, the defender is coached to deliver a blow into the center with a two-hand shiver, keeping his elbows locked and arms extended to keep the main blocker away from his body. The middle guard should keep his shoulders squared so he can get rid of the center and pursue in any direction. Therefore, he must keep leverage on the offensive center's one-on-one block, shed him, and get to the ball carrier. The "0" defender is responsible to defend from the head to head of the offensive guards (Diagram 2-1).

Explosive Charge: The middle guard must be able to look at the center's blocking technique and then kinesthetically feel the blocker with his hands, while checking the flow of the offensive backfield. If lined up off the line, the defender must deliver a forearm blow or a two-hand shiver into the center and then maintain his shoulders parallel to the line of scrimmage. To deliver a solid blow to neutralize the offensive center, the defender must drop his butt and then explode up and through the blocker to defeat the center's one-on-one block.

If the middle guard is lined up tight, crowding the offensive center, we like the "0" defender to use his two-hand shiver. He must shed the blocker as soon as possible. The defender must keep his feet moving and his shoulders squared to the line of scrimmage.

Pursuit: The middle guard's pursuit pattern must be quick and flat. Since the middle guard is head up on the center, he must be quick to be able to pursue and cut off the ball carrier from his centrally located position. The flat course is only natural, if the middle guard goes in his key's direction, and he must flatten his pursuit course to cut off the ball carrier. This is why it is most important for the middle guard to keep his shoulders squared to the line if he is to have any chance to pursue and gang-tackle the ball carrier.

Middle Guard's "0" Technique vs. Center's Cut-Off Block: Against the offensive center's cut-off block, the middle guard is coached to step in the direction of the center's head and deliver a blow with the same forearm. If the center has already cut off the middle guard, he is then coached to bring the same arm up and through the blocker in an uppercut fashion, stepping through the head of the blocker. The next step is with the backside foot, which brings the defender into a parallel stance with his shoulders squared off to the line of scrimmage. From this position, the "0" man can move up and down the line of scrimmage to cut off the ball carrier at the point of the attack.

The two-hand shiver is also used by our middle guard as part of his defensive plan of attack. The quick two-hand shiver blow helps to neutralize the center and keep the defender's shoulders parallel to the line of scrimmage.

The quicker the middle guard, the closer we align him to the ball; the slower he is, the farther we place him off the line of scrimmage. This allows the slower defender more time to key the offensive center's block and read the flow of the offensive backs.

Once the middle guard has been cut off, we teach the "0" defender to spin out opposite the blocker's pressure and shuffle or scallop down the line of scrimmage to intercept the ball carrier at the point of the offensive attack. The defensive spin-out technique is used only as a final resort, and the defender must spin out flat and as close to the line of scrimmage as possible. If the defender spins out too deeply, he opens up a seam in the defense which weakens the defensive attack considerably.

Center's Cut-Off Block: The middle guard must drive through the head of the center and cover his area to head up of the offensive guard's original position. If the center consistently attempts to scramble low, out on all fours, at times our more agile "0" defenders have used a leapfrog technique and gone right over the scrambler's head! The leapfrog technique is accomplished by the defender putting his hands on the blocker's head and shoulders (Diagram 2-2).

Center's One-on-One Block: The middle guard, from his crowded position on the center, uses a two-hand shiver. The middle guard must lock his elbows to keep the center away from his wheels and destroy the pivot man's block. The "0" defender must be able to cover the area between the heads of the offensive guards. He must move to the ball, keeping his shoulders square (Diagram 2-3).

DIAGRAM 2-2   DIAGRAM 2-3

Guard-Center's Double Team Block: The "0" defender is coached to use the anchor technique versus the double team block. The middle guard drops his outside shoulder and goes down to all fours to defend against the two-time block. Then the defender is taught to attempt to split the double team block (Diagram 2-4).

Versus the Three-Man Wedge: The defensive middle guard must quickly drop down on all fours and then whip his neck, head, and shoul-

DIAGRAM 2-4   DIAGRAM 2-5

ders up and grab as many opponents' legs as possible. The defender should anchor his position and never rise high enough to cause him to be driven backward (Diagram 2-5).

Middle Guard's "0" Technique vs. Guard's Drive Block: As soon as the guard begins to drive down on the middle guard, the defender is coached to take a short step in the blocker's direction. The defender is coached to explode his near forearm flipper into the potential blocker. The defender is coached to keep his backside arm free and then to shuffle along the line of scrimmage, fighting against the offensive blocker's pressure. His pursuit path must be set in a proper angle to cut off the ball carrier at the point of the offensive attack (Diagram 2-6).

DIAGRAM 2-6

DIAGRAM 2-7

Middle Guard's "0" Technique vs. Guard's Fold Block: Key the center's angle block by stepping forward with the near foot, and then bring the back foot up parallel to the line of scrimmage. Look for the guard's fold block as soon as the center begins his angle block path. Meet the fold blocker head on, using either the forearm flipper or the two-hand power shiver. Get rid of the blocker and get to the point of attack. The nose guard should slide right and left along the line of scrimmage, with his shoulders square to the line. Using this technique, the defender will attack the ball carrier nose on with his shoulders parallel to the goal line (Diagram 2-7).

Middle Guard's Step-Around Move: The defender must be quick and key the center's head and shoulders. The "0" defender must make sure he gets his lead and back foot all the way around, using his hands to work the legs around the center's block. The middle guard must work first for width and then react to the block of the center. If the play goes away or backside, the step around middle guard must be quick to take a flat course to cut off the ball carrier (Diagram 2-8).

The center must never be able to cut off or reach the middle guard's step-around technique.

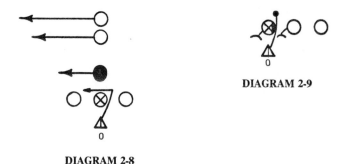

DIAGRAM 2-9

DIAGRAM 2-8

As the middle guard steps around, he must be ready for a reach block by the near offensive guard. Therefore, the step-around "0" technique must be a "rip-like" technique as close to the center as possible (Diagram 2-9).

Why the Middle Guard's Step-Around Technique: The middle guard must have the ability to initiate his own defensive move occasionally. This means that on a given signal by the middle guard to his linebackers, the "0" defender is free to use a quick defensive step-around or side step to keep the offensive blocker honest. A few successful middle guard stunts minimize the all-out fire out blocking technique used by the offensive center on the "0" man. This split-second de'ay by the blocker gives the defender the added impetus to break free of the center's block on crucial downs.

DEFENSIVE LINEBACKER'S "223" ASSIGNMENTS

The Fifty Defense must have two leaders as their linebackers. These two players can lead in any method: by work, deed, or action. We don't care if a linebacker is a chatterbox or a quiet lad, as long as he can get the job done.

One of our linebackers is selected to call the defenses. We select the Fifty linebacker because of his position in the center of our defense as a lookout for maximum offensive line splits, or to sound a vocal alert to adjust or call the direction of a particular defensive stunt or blitz.

The Fifty linebacker must be vicious versus the run. He must have excellent pursuit and gang-tackle the ball carrier from sideline to sideline. He must have the quickness and the ability to blitz through the offensive line and throw the offense for losses on key downs. The "223" defender must also be able to play pass defense and come up with that big interception in a clutch situation.

All of this means the linebacker had better be a total defender. He should be quick, strong, agile, intelligent, and most of all, a consistent hitter. Certainly with these defensive attributes, the linebacker could play defensively in any given position in the Fifty Defense.

Alignment and Depth: The defensive linebacker should line up in his normal "223" alignment, splitting the offensive guard's outside foot with the midline of his body.

The regular depth of the linebacker is slightly deeper than the heels of the defensive tackles. The linebacker is taught to crowd the line of scrimmage on short-yardage plays and play slightly deeper on long-yardage passing situations (Diagram 2-10).

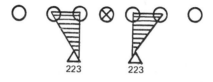

DIAGRAM 2-10

The Fifty linebacker is responsible to take away the opposition's abnormally large splits (between the offensive guard and center gap), by jumping into the "1" gap at the last moment.

Stance: The linebacker is coached to line up in a well-balanced two-point football position. His legs and shoulders should be parallel to the line of scrimmage and his knees must be bent. His arms should hang down (slightly inside his knees), ready to protect his feet and to deliver a blow to either his left or right. This means the linebacker's weight should be balanced and his weight should be equally distributed directly over the balls of his feet.

Keys: The Fifty linebacker is coached to key the near back through the head of the offensive guard. The near back could be a halfback in the normal halfback position or a tailback in the "I" offensive alignment.

Responsibilities: The defender must be ready to meet the main blocker (offensive guard) and deliver a forearm blow whether the blocker attempts to block the linebacker to the inside or the outside. The "223" defender must move on movement of the offensive guard, deliver a forearm and neutralize him, fight the blocker's pressure, pursue laterally by scalloping up and down the line of scrimmage, and gang-tackle the ball carrier.

The defender is coached to keep his outside arm free to take on any down blocks from his outside. As soon as the play develops, the defender must read the offensive blocking pattern, defeat the blockers, and take a lead step with his playside foot in the direction of the offensive play. The "223" linebacker is coached to keep his shoulders parallel to the line of scrimmage, so he can step up and meet the ball carrier in the hole, at the line of scrimmage, with his shoulders square.

He must be careful to stay a step behind the ball carrier so he does not make the mistake of overrunning the ball.

Explosive Charge: As soon as the blocker approaches or takes on the Fifty linebacker, the defender is coached to deliver a solid forearm block into the defender's numbers. We coach the Fifty linebacker to use the forearm blow whenever possible, because the forearm blow is more powerful than the two-hand shiver. The defender is coached to step first and hit second. This is a quick one-two movement (set-blow), which with continual practice becomes second nature to the defender. The blow should be taught with an upswing motion of the flipper, powered off a short step with the same foot, same arm.

How to Deliver the Forearm Blow: The defender's fist must be clenched and the arm should be bent at the elbow; the hitting area is the hard or bone part of the defensive player's forearm. The defensive player is coached to concentrate on the target area just at the bottom of the offensive player's numbers. The small finger of the forearm should be turned slightly upward to increase the power and strength of the upward lift.

The powerful lead step with the near foot and the upward lift of the near forearm should strike the opponent and the ground almost simultaneously. The striking defender is coached to bend his knees so he can spring or explode out and up through his opponent when delivering this powerful forearm lift. As soon as the inside forearm is triggered, the other arm should be brought up to protect the defender's blind side and to help get rid of the neutralized defender. Thus, the outside free arm will feel the pressure of any potential double team blocker. If pressure (blocking pressure) comes from the double team side, the defender should step toward this drive blocker and hit with the same arm into the opponent.

Pursuit: When play goes to the Fifty linebacker's side, he is coached to pursue down the line of scrimmage, scalloping, checking each. hole to take on the ball carrier with the defender's shoulders squared to the line of scrimmage.

If the play goes away, the Fifty linebacker is coached to take a set step and check for any possible counter plays before taking his proper pursuit angle. The angle of the "223" defender's pursuit depends upon where the ball carrier is running, the ball carrier's speed, and the speed of the defender. Naturally, the Fifty defender is coached, just the same as his other ten defensive teammates, never to follow a jersey the same color as his in pursuing the ball.

One-on-One Block by Guard: Meet the offensive guard head on, stepping with the inside foot, delivering with the inside forearm, and destroying the guard's block (Diagram 2-11).

DIAGRAM 2-11

DIAGRAM 2-12

Reach Block by Guard: The defensive linebacker must never get hooked. Fight through the blocker's head and scallop to the original position of your fellow linebacker, looking quickly for the off-tackle hole (Diagram 2-12).

Tackle's Drive Block: The "223" backer must keep his outside arm free to protect against the offensive tackle's down block. The defender must look for this block versus Triple Option football teams. Fight through the tackle's head and scallop to the off-tackle hole (Diagram 2-13).

One on One vs. the Center: On some trap plays, the offensive center may try to block back on the linebacker, and he must fight through

DIAGRAM 2-13

DIAGRAM 2-14

the pivot man's head, fighting pressure, and begin his scallop pursuit course (Diagram 2-14).

Halfback Isolation Block: As soon as the offensive guard blocks down and the offensive tackle turns out, we coach the linebacker to look for the isolation block. We want the "223" defender stepping up and stuffing the iso-blocker right back into the ball carrier's lap. This is referred to as the linebacker reading the blocking pattern and attacking the main blocker (Diagram 2-15).

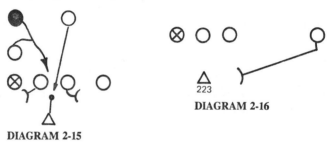

DIAGRAM 2-16

DIAGRAM 2-15

Crackback Block by the Split End: As soon as the split end takes his position, we want the linebacker to think "Crackback." The outside secondary defender is coached to yell, "Crack, crack, crack!" but the "223" defender must be always ready for this block to the split side (Diagram 2-16).

Guard Pulls: Whenever the guard pulls in any direction, the linebacker must first check for the false key (quick give to the drive back naked over the pulling guard's vacated area). If there is no false key, the linebacker then begins to mirror the pulling guard, checking the offensive blocking pattern as he moves (Diagram 2-17). The linebacker must be careful not to overrun the ball carrier. This is why we tell the linebacker to stay one step behind the ball carrier, because the defender is still deep enough to come up and tackle the ball carrier on the line of scrimmage (Diagram 2-17).

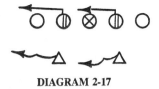

DIAGRAM 2-17

DEFENSIVE TACKLE'S "45" ASSIGNMENTS

The defensive tackle's main role is to anchor the Fifty Defense. This defender must be strong enough to fight off the double team block and quick enough to give a competent pass rush. The "45" defender must be coached never to get hooked or be turned out by the offensive tackle. At times, the defender must be quick enough to defeat the offensive guard when the defensive tackle has been "knocked down" to the split end's side.

Alignment and Stance: The defensive tackle is first taught to crowd the line of scrimmage, so he can deliver a forearm flipper into the main offensive blocker immediately. Then, at times, the defensive tackle may be moved two feet off the line of scrimmage in order to read the blocking patterns of the offensive line. The defensive call, down, and distance offensive tendencies often determine the depth the "45" defender will be taught to play off the line of scrimmage. This defender is coached to split the offensive tackle's outside foot with the midline of the defensive tackle's body. If the offensive lineman takes a maximum split, the defensive tackle is coached to jump into the "3" gap and shoot to the inside as quickly as possible (Diagram 2-18).

DIAGRAM 2-18

Defensive Tackle's Alignment "45" Depth: Our rookie tackles are coached to line up in their normal "45" alignments and as close to the line of scrimmage as possible. This tight alignment is continued until both the coach and the player realize that the defender is not quick enough to read and react to the offensive line's blocking techniques from this posi-

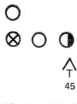

DIAGRAM 2-19

tion. When this happens, the "45" defender is coached to move off the line of scrimmage, so he is able to confidently and consistently defeat the offensive blocking techniques and cut off the ball carrier at the point of attack (Diagram 2-19).

The depth of the defender is often the most overlooked coaching point in coaching defensive line play.

Stance: All of our inexperienced tackles are coached to begin in a four-point defensive stance. The other tackles may elect to use a three-point stance if they prove successful in this stance. If moved off the line two feet in a reading depth, the defensive tackle is coached to lift his head slightly and drop his butt so he can key and read the offensive tackle.

When crowding the line of scrimmage, the "45" defender is taught to stay as low as possible, keeping his feet up under his body so he can quickly uncoil into action. The feet should be apart about the width of his armpits. His hands should be placed parallel about one and one-half feet in front of his forward foot.

Key: The defensive tackle who is responsible for crowding the line of scrimmage keys the offensive tackle's near down hand and shoulder, because in his crowded alignment, it is most difficult to key his head which is normally lower than his hips.

When the "45" defender lines up two to three feet off the line of scrimmage, he lifts his head up and his hips have a tendency to drop lower than his head. Thus, the defensive tackle now keys the head of the offensive tackle. If the offensive tackle's head goes to the inside, the defensive tackle should begin to close down to the inside, keeping his outside arm free for any potential block from the outside. The defensive tackle must never get hooked by the offensive tackle and should immediately shuffle to the outside whenever the offensive tackle's head goes to the outside of the "45" defender.

Whenever the defensive tackle has crowded the ball and has difficulty reading his key, he is coached to move off the line a couple of feet until he can more easily read his offensive key.

Explosive Charge: The defensive tackle is coached to move on his offensive key's movement and to deliver a neutralizing blow into the main blocker whenever his key attempts to block the "45" defender on a one-on-one block. The defender is coached to take a short six-inch step with the inside foot and deliver a blow with the inside forearm. He must step with the same foot he delivers the blow with. The defensive tackle must get his forearm flipper up and under the main blocker's number and must bring up his back foot to square his shoulders to the line of scrimmage. This is a most important follow-through phase of the defensive charge because the anchoring defensive tackle may be attacked by a blocker from another angle at any time. The defender's backside arm must be ready to take on an outside blocker or to get rid of the one-on-one block by the main offensive blocker.

The defensive tackle must stay low and fight the pressure of the block, so he may quickly get into his prescribed pursuit angle. The defender's follow-through and shuffle should always leave the defender's shoulders parallel to the line of scrimmage.

Responsibilities: If no one blocks the defensive tackle, he must penetrate approximately one yard (unless a pass shows) and look for a possible inside-out trap block technique by a potential inside offensive blocker. He must maintain a square shoulder position and be prepared to pursue in any direction, once he picks up the flow of the ball.

Whenever the offensive tackle takes a maximum split, the defensive tackle has the option of jumping into that gap and shooting the gap to the inside. The "45" defender does not jump into the gap until the offensive tackle gets down into his offensive stance. Now the offensive tackle cannot move, and, at the last second, the "45" defender jumps into the gap and shoots across before the offensive tackle can get a piece of him.

Use of Hands for Defensive Tackle: The defender is coached to use his hands on all blocks other than the base block. If the defensive tackle is being hooked, cut off, or reach blocked, he is coached to go to the potential blocker's far shoulder with his hands to keep the defender's far leg free. A quick step with the near foot and a quick sliding step with the back side foot helps to keep the defensive tackle's feet and shoulders square to the line of scrimmage. At times, we teach him to chug or jam the potential blocker's release to keep him from blocking our linebacker.

Use of Defensive Tackle's Hands During Pass Rush: The defensive tackle must have quick hands and fast feet versus the offensive pass-blocking techniques. The tackle's quick feet help to get a jump on the blocker and his hands help him to turn the blocker's shoulders perpendicular to the line of scrimmage. As long as the blocker's shoulders are not parallel to the line of scrimmage, the defensive tackle has a much greater chance of rushing the passer. To turn the blocker's shoulders, the defensive tackle is taught to use the push-pull or the butt-pull method to throw the blocker's timing off.

Pursuit: The Fifty defensive tackles must keep their shoulders parallel to the line of scrimmage as they begin their pursuit courses. The reason for this technique is to be able to defend against the quick cut-back play or the quick offensive counter plays. Once the ball goes away and crosses the line of scrimmage, the defensive tackle must forget trying to maintain his squared shoulders and must sprint to his proper deep angle to cut off the ball carrier. The "45" defender is told never to follow the same color jersey. This means that if one of the tackle's teammates is ahead of him, he should take a deeper angle and continue to pursue.

Defensive Tackle's Anticipated Pass Rush: Whenever our defensive tackle expects a pass, the defender is coached to adjust his defensive four-point stance. This means the defensive tackle is coached to narrow down his feet so he can explode quicker from this defensive pass rush stance. This narrowed stance helps the defender to get off his mark quicker than he can from his normal defensive stance.

Defensive Linemen's Slant Charge: Our defensive linemen are coached to slant down through the head of the blocker. If the blocker attempts to use the turn-out block, the defender is coached to barrel directly through the head of the potential blocker. All of our defenders are coached to read the blocking techniques and patterns on the move and to use their hands to ward off the potential blockers. The slanting defender must be coached to stay low and expect the blocker to step his way immediately.

Techniques "45": The defensive tackle must be able to defeat the offensive tackle on a one-on-one basis, using either his forearm flipper or two-hand shiver. The "45" defender must be coached to hit and shed the

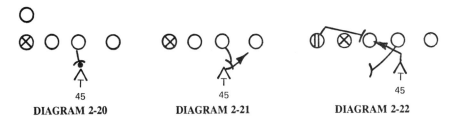

| DIAGRAM 2-20 | DIAGRAM 2-21 | DIAGRAM 2-22 |

blocker quickly, pursue, and then react and tackle the ball carrier (Diagram 2-20).

Whenever the offensive tackle attempts to reach block or hook the defensive tackle, the defender is taught to use his two-hand shiver, keep leverage on the defender, and slide to the outside, keeping his shoulders parallel to the line of scrimmage (Diagram 2-21).

Whenever a trap shows, the defensive tackle must close down and meet the trapper with his shoulders parallel to the line of scrimmage. The defender should power into the inside-out trapper with his inside forearm and shoulder. The "45" defender must drive off his back foot and attack the trapper (Diagram 2-22).

Defensive Tackle versus the Double Team Block: We want our defensive tackle to defeat the post block first and then attack the drive block's pressure second. The defensive tackle must first be an anchor and not allow the double teaming blockers to drive him backward and cut off our defensive pursuit. The defender must fire out on movement and explode into the post blocker. He is taught to wedge his shoulders between the blockers and split the double team block whenever possible. If he is being moved backward, he is coached to go down to all fours and anchor his position. As a last resort, he is taught to spin or roll out in reverse direction away from the drive blocker's pressure. The spin-out technique must be flat so as not to open up a seam in the defensive front and not to cut off defensive pursuit (Diagram 2-23).

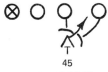

DIAGRAM 2-23

Defensive Spin-Out Technique: The spin-out technique is used by our defender only as a last resort. This means the defender's pursuit attack (correct angle) has been cut off by the blocker's angle. The defender is coached to pivot off the near foot, closest to the blocker, throwing the opposite arm and leg around and back toward the potential blocker. Once the spin has been completed, the defender should have his shoulders square to the line of scrimmage and should have gained his proper pursuit angle on the ball carrier.

If the blocker is still maintaining his block, the defender steps away from the blocker with the outside foot, using his arms to ward off the blocker. The defender should continue to shuffle away from the blocker.

The defender must be careful to:

1. Spin out as close (flat) to the line of scrimmage as possible.
2. Push the blocker away and never pull the blocker across his body when trying to get rid of him (Diagram 2-24).

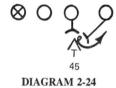

DIAGRAM 2-24

DEFENSIVE END'S "67" ASSIGNMENT

The defensive end is asked to do more things than any other defensive player in the Fifty Defense. The "67" defender must be a two-point pure end, a defensive tackle in a four-point stance, or a defender asked to play a linebacker's position in a two-point stance off the line of scrimmage. The defensive end thus becomes the Fifty Defense's Jack of all trades.

Alignment and Depth: The "67" defensive end lines up splitting the offensive end's outside foot with the midline of the defender's body.

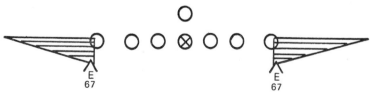

DIAGRAM 2-25

Normally the defender crowds the line of scrimmage as close as possible. The specific depth of the defender's position is dependent upon the defense or stunt called (Diagram 2-25).

Stance: The defensive end is coached to line up in a two-point stance with the near foot up and the outside foot back in a toe-to-instep alignment. He should line up in a two-point football position with his arms hanging loosely in front of his knees. The defensive end's knees should be bent slightly so he can explode into the main offensive blocker.

Key: The "67" defender is taught to key the offensive end's helmet and through to the near offensive back.

Responsibilities: The defensive end must stop the off-tackle play first and must be able to react to the sweep, forcing the play wide into the defensive secondary contain man. He must be ready to contain the reverse and counter plays. At times, the defensive end must be ready to defend against the pass by dropping off the line of scrimmage to defend his flat area. If the play goes away, he must check for counter or reverse and then take a deep pursuit angle to cut off the ball carrier.

Explosive Charge: The defensive end should explode forward with a short jab step with the front foot, and be ready to deliver a blow with the inside arm into the blocker. This means the defensive end must pick out his "main man." The "main man" is the most important blocker who is assigned to block the "67" defender. The defensive end must deliver a flipper under and into the blocker's numbers. As the defensive end fights pressure, he should get rid of the main blocker by pushing him inside toward the ball carrier's route. This means he must fight through the blocker's pressure by driving through the blocker's head.

The defensive end must never be hooked; thus, he must be ready to take a flat step to the outside with the back foot and shuffle the front foot in the same direction. We refer to this as "hiding the outside foot." As he shuffles to the outside, he should ward off the blocker with his two hands. The defender must keep his balance and maintain his shoulders parallel to the line of scrimmage as much as possible.

The defensive "67" end must read the near offensive back for a hook block or a kick-out block. At times, the offensive back will employ a low scramble block on the "67" defender. One technique we like our end to use against this scramble block is to leapfrog over this blocker and attack the ball carrier "right now!"

If the offense tries to kick out, to cross block or trap the defensive end, the defender is coached to meet this inside-out block with his shoulders parallel to the line of scrimmage. This allows the defender to anchor his outside leg and deliver a forearm and shoulder blow into the defender. Again the defensive end must be coached to step to the inside with his inside foot to help explode and neutralize the potential blocker.

If a sweep should develop, the defensive end must get rid of the blocker as soon as possible and scallop to the outside in a shuffling manner to force the sweep to the outside. If the "67" defender can gain a one and one-half yard depth into the opposition's backfield, the chances of a gain have been minimized.

Regardless of whether the defensive end fights off the main blocker with a forearm blow, two-hand shiver, or leapfrog over the scrambling blocker, the "67" defender must defeat the blocker first and then tackle the ball carrier.

Pursuit Course: The defensive end is coached to hold and check for a counter, bootleg, or reverse before taking a deep pursuit course to head off the ball carrier. The pursuing defender is coached never to follow the same color jersey and always to take a slightly deeper pursuit course than the nearest pursuing defender.

Defending Against the End's Hook Block: The first thing we teach our defensive end in the Fifty Defense is *never get hooked*. Since he is reading the offensive end's helmet, the defender is coached to take a parallel step with the outside foot so he cannot be hooked. This is called "hiding the outside foot." As the defensive end steps to the outside with the far foot, he is taught to use a straight-arm two-hand shiver. The inside arm pushes off the potential blocker's helmet and outside shoulder. The reason the defender is coached to use his straight-arm, elbows-locked shiver is to keep the blocker away from the "67" defender's feet. The defender must get rid of the potential blocker completely before he takes on the ball carrier or the next blocker. The defender must be ready to lose ground if necessary to avoid being hooked by the near offensive linemen.

Once the defender is hooked, as a last resort, he is coached to pivot out or whirl out against pressure to force the ball carrier to the inside. As soon as the defender clears the hook block, he must maintain his shoulders square to the line of scrimmage so he can defeat the next blocker or tackle the approaching ball carrier.

The hook block is usually used by an offense which features fast

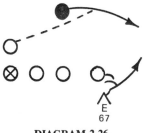

DIAGRAM 2-26

backs, who have a tendency to sweep to the wide side of the field. Some running attacks use a quick sweep attack to the short side of the field often as a built-in running series to augment their two-minute stop-the-clock passing attack. The defensive end's key, off the helmet of the offensive end through to the near back, helps to read the quick sweep and contain this potentially explosive play (Diagram 2-26).

Defending Against the Turn-Out Block: As soon as the defender keys the offensive end's helmet turning out in the first stage of the turn-out block, the "67" defender is coached to step toward the blocker with his inside foot and use his forearm flipper to drive straight through the blocker's head. The defensive end is cautioned never to go around to the inside of the head of the blocker, because he will be too late to tackle the ball carrier. The defender must step down with the backside foot and close off the off-tackle hole with his shoulders parallel to the line of scrimmage (Diagram 2-27).

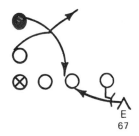

DIAGRAM 2-27

The turn-out block is usually used on a quick thrust-off tackle, a dive, or some type of inside trap play. The inside power play is usually used in short "must" yardage plays. Therefore, on third down and short-yardage plays the defensive end should be alert for one of these quick-hitting inside running plays.

Defending Against the Trap Block: Normally the offensive end will release toward the inside, and the offensive frontside or backside guard will pull and trap the ''67'' defender, using an inside-out trap block. The defensive end is coached to step down with the near foot and push the releasing end down to the inside with his inside hand on the end's outside hip and the outside hand on the end's butt. As soon as the ''67'' defender steps to the inside with the near foot, he should shuffle his backside foot down to the inside. The defender's shoulders should be squared to the line of scrimmage and most of the defensive end's weight should be on the inside foot, in order to meet the inside-out trap block with maximum power and force. The defensive end must stay low and close down in to the trapper, meeting the blocker with the powerful blast of the inside forearm and shoulder blast. The defensive blow must be delivered low under the potential trapper's pads, driving low and following up through the blocker's body. This maintains defensive leverage on the inside-out trap blocker. The defender is taught to go after the trapper as quickly as possible to minimize the trap hole. The defensive end must keep his head up and not try to use it in taking on the trapper. When this happens, the ''67'' defender often misses the tackle because his vision is impaired by the blow to the defender's head (Diagram 2-28).

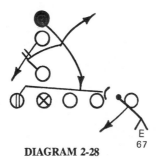

DIAGRAM 2-28

The trapping game is usually run against a penetrating defense. A solid trapping offense usually has an outstanding ground attack, because it takes a sound coaching staff to institute a successful trapping game. Some offensive teams have a tendency to trap on long-yardage potential pass plays. Offensive tendencies obtained from scouting reports and opponents' game films usually give our defensive ends a feeling for when the opposition favors their trapping game.

Defending Against the Halfback Hook Block: Whenever the offensive end releases or blocks down to the inside, the defensive end is coached to begin to close down to the inside, but first to read the path of the near offensive back. As soon as the near back begins an arc-like route to hook the defensive end, the defender must shift his body weight to the outside and fight outside the head of the potential hook blocker. Generally, the path of the near back telegraphs an outside maneuver by the offense. As the defender steps to the outside, he should use a "rip technique" and bring his inside arm up and through the near back's outside shoulder, so the "67" defender will end up with his shoulders level to the line of scrimmage and in an excellent defensive football position to attack the ball carrier.

The "rip technique" takes the defensive end outside, but not too far outside, which might open up a hole to run inside the "67" defender's defensive path (Diagram 2-29).

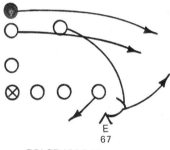

DIAGRAM 2-29

The near back's hook block technique usually signals sweep for the defensive end, which may occur on any offensive play. The defender must also realize he must read the flow of the ball, because some offensive attacks use the near back's arc path to set up the trap play to run inside the defensive end.

Defending Against the Cross Block: As soon as the offensive end blocks down, the defensive end must be ready for a cross block from the near side offensive tackle. The "67" defender must meet the offensive tackle low, with his shoulders squared to the line of scrimmage. We coach the defensive end to close down to the inside as quickly as possible, so he can deliver on the offensive cross blocker before the tackle can gain any momentum toward the defender. Against the larger and stronger offensive tackles, our coaching staff encourages the defensive end to step into the tackle low with the inside shoulder and forearm blow. The defensive end must bend his knees to explode with all of his power into the inside-out blocker.

Once the blocker has delivered on the "67" defender, the end must fight through the head of the blocker to stop the quick-hitting offensive play (Diagram 2-30).

Usually the offense runs this play when it does not have a lead back to the side of the tight end. (*Example*: the Pro I Attack illustrated in Diagram 2-30.) The cross block is also used whenever the offense chooses not to use an inside-out trap block by a pulling guard.

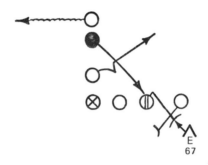

DIAGRAM 2-30

Defending Against the Back's Kick-Out Block: The defender must look inside for a back to kick or block him out as quickly as he closes down, with the offensive end's down-blocking path. Just as against the inside-out trap block, the defender closes down with his shoulders parallel to the line of scrimmage and takes on the blocking back, with his inside flipper using the same foot same shoulder pattern. The "67" defender is coached to squeeze down the off-tackle hole, forcing the ball carrier back toward the inside defensive pursuit. The defensive end must be taught never to go around the blocker, but to fight directly through the head of the blocking back, to intercept the ball carrier behind or on the line of scrimmage.

This off-tackle play has been used successfully when the fullback kicks out the defensive end off the power double team block, with the I-back curling up and into the off-tackle hole (Diagram 2-31). The "67" defender can easily key this block because of the emphasized path of the inside-out angle of the near back in the "I."

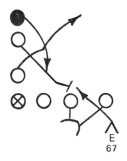

DIAGRAM 2-31

3

The Stunting Fifty Defense

We stunt and blitz our defenders in an attempt to force the offensive attack into committing both mental and physical errors. Blitzes and stunts are strategically called to tackle the offense for a loss and place our opponents into key second or third down and long-yardage situations. To penetrate the offensive line, we use a number of blitzing, looping, slanting, angling, and ripping techniques. Successful stunting defenses force quick turnovers and the defense goes from defense to offense quickly by forcing a fumble or pass interception.

The Fifty Loop and Fifty Safety Blitzes, discussed and diagrammed in this chapter, have been very successful against both running and passing attacks. The Fifty Blast and Double Blast are keyed upon the tailback's directional course, and his movement determines when, where, and if our linebackers will blitz.

FIFTY LOOP RINGO

Whenever this stunt is called, it is a key for our entire defensive front to loop to the Ringo (right) side. This is one of our favorite stunts, because we can easily disguise it by lining up in our normal Fifty alignment. The defenders are coached to take a quick 45 degree step to their right with the near foot and then a crossover step with the backside foot. As the defenders hit their respective gaps, they are coached to drop their shoulders and bring the backside arm up and through to prevent the blocker's head from cutting off our defenders.

This seven-man stunt fills all of the defensive gaps and still maintains our four-step secondary defense. This is an excellent call whenever we wish to penetrate and force the opposition into a bad play. We like to use this stunt inside our forty-yard line or in our opponent's four-down territory. Fifty Loop Ringo has been an excellent second down and long situation, because it also gives our defense an excellent rush when the opposition decides to pass on second down (Diagram 3-1).

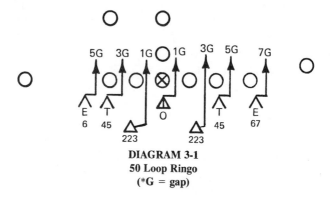

DIAGRAM 3-1
50 Loop Ringo
(*G = gap)

ALIGNMENT AND STUNT (LOOP RINGO)

Left End—Lines up in a "67" alignment and loops to his right into a "5" gap assignment.

Left Tackle—Lines up in a "45" alignment and loops to his right into a "3" gap assignment.

Left Inside Linebacker—Lines up in a "223" alignment and loops to his right into a "1" gap assignment.

Middle Guard—Lines up in his "0" alignment and loops to his right into a "1" gap assignment.

Right Inside Linebacker—Lines up in a "223" alignment and loops to his right into a "3" gap assignment.

Right Tackle—Lines up into a "45" alignment and loops to his right into a "5" gap assignment.

Right End—Lines up in a "67" alignment and loops to his right into a "7" assignment.

Generally, we use a straight man-to-man pass defense whenever we employ a seven-man stunt. The cornerbacks are assigned the widest receivers to their side and the defensive safeties pick up the next widest receivers to their side (Diagram 3-1).

FIFTY SAFETY BLITZ (RINGO)

We rush eight and run a three-deep secondary defense when we want an all-out rush on a predetermined passing down. We will also rush eight when we expect a run on a second down and four or five yards to go. The eight-man rush is especially good versus a two-tight-end offense, because the defense needs eight men to cover all the gaps.

Whenever the safety blitz is called, all the defensive ends, tackles, and linebackers execute a loop to their outside. The middle guard loops to his right to the side of the call (Ringo), and the backside (weakside) safetyman is assigned to use his safety blitz technique through the one gap. All of the remaining defensive safetymen use their respective man-to-man defensive assignments (Diagram 3-2).

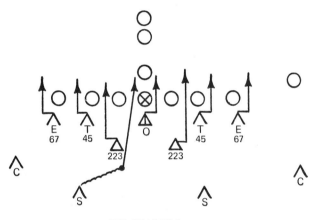

DIAGRAM 3-2
50 Safety Blitz Ringo

ALIGNMENT AND STUNT (SAFETY BLITZ RINGO)

Left End—Lines up in a "67" alignment and loops to his left into a "7" assignment.

Left Tackle—Lines up in a "45" alignment and loops to his left into a "5" gap assignment.

Left Inside Linebacker—Lines up in a "223" alignment and loops to his left into a "3" gap assignment.

Middle Guard—Lines up in a "0" alignment and loops to his right into a "1" gap assignment.

Right Inside Linebacker—Lines up in a "223" alignment and loops to his right into a "3" gap alignment.

Right Tackle—Lines up in a "45" alignment and loops to his right into a "5" gap alignment.

Right End—Lines up in a "67" alignment and loops to his right into a "7" alignment.

Left Safetyman—Lines up in his normal position and gets a running start just prior to the center's snap and blitzes into the one remaining open "1" gap.

One important coaching point for all of our stunting linemen and blitzing linebackers or defensive backs is that they are coached never to disguise their alignments to the point where they cannot get to their blitzing or stunting areas. Thus, if one of our defensive linemen realizes he cannot stunt or loop from an outside shoulder position into an inside gap area, he is coached to employ a more realistic (head-up) alignment so he is able to get to his assigned position once the ball has been put into play (Diagram 3-2).

FIFTY BLAST LUCKY

Whenever we call our Blast Stunt, we normally key a particular offensive back and the left linebacker blitzes into the opposite one gap whenever the key goes away from this linebacker. The middle guard loops to the side of the Lucky (left) call into the "1" gap. The right linebacker keys his near side guard-back key and plays his normal "223" linebacker assignment. All of the other defenders play their normal Fifty techniques (Diagram 3-3).

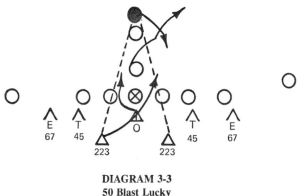

DIAGRAM 3-3
50 Blast Lucky

If the key (I-back) comes to the side of the call, the middle guard still loops to the Lucky side into his "1" gap assignment. The left linebacker keys the I-Back and scrapes off into the "3" gap area. This move by the I-Back brings both the middle guard and left linebacker quickly to the correct side of the point of the attack. All of the other defensive players play their normal Fifty assignments (Diagram 3-4).

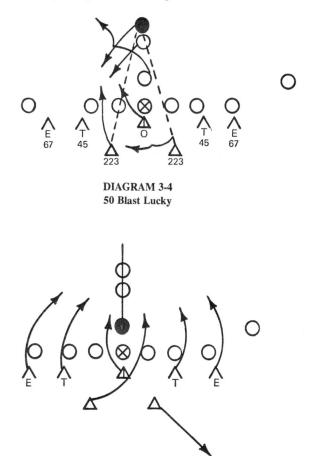

DIAGRAM 3-4
50 Blast Lucky

DIAGRAM 3-5
50 Blast Lucky vs. Drop-Back Pass

If a drop-back pass shows by the quarterback, the blitz is still on, with the left linebacker blitzing through the opposite "1" gap, and the middle guard loops to his left carrying out his normal Blast Lucky assignment. The other defensive linemen use their normal pass rushes when a drop-back pass shows. The right inside linebacker drops back into his regular hook zone assignment. All six of the pass rushes must maintain their correct pass rush lanes (Diagram 3-5).

FIFTY DOUBLE BLAST LUCKY

The Double Blast means two linebackers will blitz rather than only one Fifty linebacker as in Blast Lucky. If the key goes away from the call, away from the middle guard's left loop, the backside linebacker is assigned to loop into the opposite "1" gap, while the right linebacker is coached to scrape off through the "3" gap. (See the solid lines in Diagram 3-6.)

If the key (I-back) goes toward the Lucky (left) side, the left linebacker checks the "3" gap to his side and the backside linebacker plays his normal Fifty defense, checking first for the counter; then he begins to scallop toward the ball, checking each gap as he scallops or shuffles toward the ball. The middle guard loops to his left as normal, then takes a flat course to cut off the ball carrier. (See dotted lines in Diagram 3-6.)

DIAGRAM 3-6
50 Double Blast Lucky

FIFTY STING LUCKY

The Fifty Sting Lucky Stunt features a strong four-man rush to the offensive attack's strong side. The directional Lucky call is necessary to tell the linebackers which way to go. This is a particularly strong rush versus the sprint-out passing attacks or the back-up passing game.

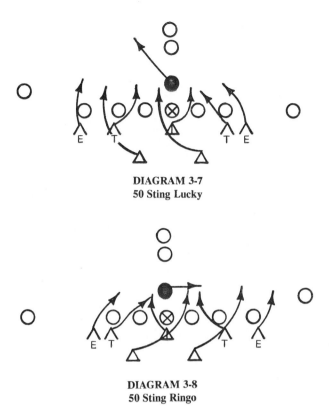

DIAGRAM 3-7
50 Sting Lucky

DIAGRAM 3-8
50 Sting Ringo

We like the sting stunt because it is an all-out seven-man rush with both our Fifty linebackers blitzing to the same side. This is a new stunt, and it has confused a number of blocking assignments because of its surprise feature (Diagram 3-7).

If the opposition lines up with a strong set to the defense's right side, our signal caller would make a Ringo or right call. Fifty Sting Ringo would look like Diagram 3-8.

FIFTY KNOCKDOWN DEFENSE

If our defensive captain were to call for a knockdown defense, it would be in effect only to the split end's side. If the opponent's offense did not line up with a split end in its offensive formation, we would play a normal Fifty Defense. When the split end shows, our "223" linebacker moves out to a "6" alignment and knocks his weakside defensive tackle

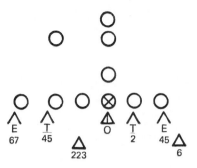

DIAGRAM 3-9

down to a "2" alignment; the defensive end is knocked down to a "45" alignment and our defense looks like Diagram 3-9.

FIFTY-ONE KNOCKDOWN

The Fifty-one Knockdown designates a defensive alignment like Diagram 3-9, and the "one" signifies a one stunt. The one linebacker is our split side linebacker in the "6" alignment. He blitzes into the "3" gap as the "2" defender loops into the "1" gap, and the "45" defender steps outside (Diagram 3-10).

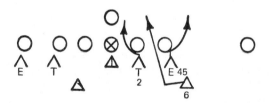

DIAGRAM 3-10

If we were aligned in a Revert alignment (Chapter 7), the linebacker would still blitz into the "3" gap (Diagram 3-11). This would be called Fifty-one Revert.

These two blitzes, Fifty-one Knockdown and Fifty-one Revert, can be switched; this means the defensive end in both the stunts would exchange his stunting assignment with the blitzing linebacker, which would result in the following Fifty-one Knockdown Switch (Diagram 3-12).

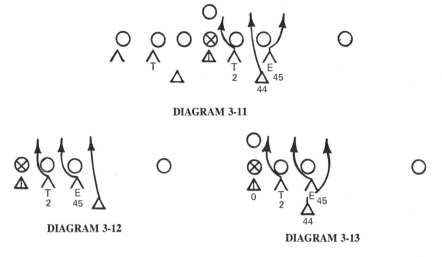

DIAGRAM 3-11

DIAGRAM 3-12

DIAGRAM 3-13

The Fifty-one Revert Switch would look like Diagram 3-13. The Revert linebacker blitzes to his "45" area, and the defensive end stunts into the "3" gap. Additional Fifty Stunts may be found under Fifty Bubble Stunts in Chapter 7.

THE FIFTY ATTACKING DEFENSE

The attacking defense often makes the big play and turns over the momentum to the offensive unit. Therefore, many attacking defenses cause more upsets in modern football than the offensive attack.

The attacking defense can score in football in more ways than the offense can. The defense has the ability to:

1. Return a kick for a touchdown.
2. Block a kick and recover it for a score.
3. Intercept a pass and return it for a touchdown.
4. Force a fumble, catch it in the air, and score.

While many defensive stunts are nothing but an exchange of defensive assignments and responsibilities, the quick change of pace often throws off the backfield's timing or the offensive line's blocking assignments. The quick linebacker's surprise blitz stunt often fires the defensive linebacker clean into the offensive backfield without even being touched by an offensive blocker. As long as the blitzing linebacker is able to conceal his red-dogging intentions, his stunting success is greatly increased.

We use defensive stunts to confuse our opponents and as a change-up from our normal reading defensive techniques. A well-executed stunt throws off the offensive blocking assignments and also often throws the offense backward for a strategic loss. This loss often forces the offense into a strategic defensive situation. (Example: second or third down and long situation.)

The attacking defense often forces the offense into many of the following errors:

1. Throwing an intercepted pass.
2. Fumbling the ball.
3. Offensive penalty.
4. Missing an offensive player's assignment.

WHEN TO BLITZ

A successful blitz on an unexpected down can put the offense in a hole, bringing up a second and fourteen or third and sixteen situation. But to blitz strategically, the linebacker should shoot from a defensive alignment where defenders are normally aligned, so that they can cut off the offensive blockers. This three-on-two ratio usually makes the big play at the right time for the defense.

WHY WE STUNT

There are many reasons for stunting and blitzing, like changing the tempo of the game, taking advantage of offensive blocking assignments, mixing up the defensive strategic pattern, and putting pressure on the passer.

WHY WE BLITZ

We like to blitz to surprise the offensive blockers. A well-coordinated blitzing defense is the most difficult defense to block. Different blitzes keep the offensive blocker thinking, and take advantage of what the defensive personnel does best. Consistent blitzing success adds to high defensive morale. A clever strategic stunting and blitzing front and secondary can change the tempo of the game and give the game momentum to the defensive eleven.

FIFTY LINEBACKER'S BLITZING TECHNIQUES

The Fifty blitzing linebacker cannot be an indecisive defender, and he must be clever enough to conceal his firing intentions. He should not give away his blitzing intentions by his crowded alignment or by his adjusted blitzing stance. The linebacker must be able to dip his inside shoulder to shoot the gap, bring up his inside arm to protect the crossover step, keep his body small and low to wedge through the smallest opening, and blitz on the snap of the ball. The Fifty blitzer must be quick and agile enough to shoot past the potential blocker, so that the shooting linebacker is not knocked off his feet or blocked off balance. Once he has penetrated the offensive gap, he must come under control, locate the ball, and be ready to take a flat pursuit course if the ball goes away from his assigned blitz course. He must be able to quickly accelerate his speed as soon as a pass shows and must use the straight path to rush the passer.

A great many coaching hours must be spent to teach the blitzing linebacker to flatten out his course if the play goes away, and shoot for angles to cut off the ball instead of running rainbows (arcs).

STUNTING AND BLITZING FILM HIGHLIGHTS

The finest method we have found to teach and sell our defenders on stunting and blitzing assignments and techniques is the use of film highlights, which we use to point out to our defenders what to do and what not to do. Since we use our own film clips, they have a greater meaning for our players, because the film shows our defenses and our opponent's offensive assignments, and features the viewers themselves or last year's teammates.

Stunting and blitzing maneuvers are done after the ball has been put into play. We also use a term, "stemming," which refers to defenders moving just prior to the snap of the ball. It is described in the following manner.

WHAT IS A STEMMING DEFENSE?

This is a strategic maneuver that lines up showing the offense one defensive alignment; and then, on a given signal, the defense stems or jumps into another defensive alignment just prior to the snap of the ball. Therefore, a stemming defense is the same as a jumping or shifting defense.

WHEN DO WE STEM?

We stem at the last moment just as the offensive quarterback begins his cadence. This means we must scout the offensive cadence with a stopwatch, if we cannot get down on the field close enough to get the exact audible sound. As long as our defensive captain has a time count, he can verbalize a signal loud enough for all of our defensive players to stem in unison. If we have a stem called and the opposition lines up in a unique offensive formation, our signal caller simply yells "Check 50!" and we jump into our normal alignment, which can adjust to any given offensive formation from the "T" to a Pro Split formation. But normally we know the opposition's basic formations through scouting reports and film exchange, and our pre-game practice sessions have been organized to stem from one defense to another to take away a particular offensive maneuver.

WHAT DEFENSES DO WE STEM TO?

Basically we line up in a normal Fifty Odd Defense and stem to another Fifty Odd or possibly a Fifty Even Defense. At times we line up in a normal Fifty Defense and stem back into a regular Fifty Defense! We like to stem from an off-the-line alignment to a crowded alignment, because our defenders are moving north and south rather than just laterally. We do not just stem from our basic Fifty Defense, because our opponents may then be able to zero in on our defensive stems. Therefore, we stem from any given defense to any defense in our defensive repertoire.

HOW FAR DO OUR DEFENDERS STEM?

Normally, we like to stem from an inside to an over or to an outside alignment to any of these three alignments. As previously stated, we favor stunting from a depth off the line of scrimmage to the same or usually to a crowded alignment in depth. These basic stems help to minimize the quick counts by the opposition's quarterback, trying to catch the defense in the act of stemming. Regardless of whether the defense is set or in the process of the stem, the offense still has to successfully execute their blocking assignments and techniques and correctly carry out their mental assignments.

FIFTY INTERIOR STEMS AND BLITZES

We like to stem and blitz our interior middle guard and linebackers in our Fifty Defenses. These three defenders are closely aligned and have a straight direct course for the quarterback's ball-handling area and dropback pass pocket.

We like to line up in the Fifty Bubble Defense (Diagram 3-14) and stem to a Fifty Defense (Diagram 3-15), or stem from a Fifty Bubble Defense (Diagram 3-14) to a Fifty Gap Stack Lucky Defense (Diagram 3-16).

If we wanted to stem into any one of these previously discussed defenses and call a Blast Lucky Stunt, these stunts would look like this: Fifty Defense-Blast Lucky (Diagram 3-17), Fifty Bubble Defense-Blast Lucky (Diagram 3-18), Fifty Gap Stack Lucky-Blast Lucky (Diagram 3-19).

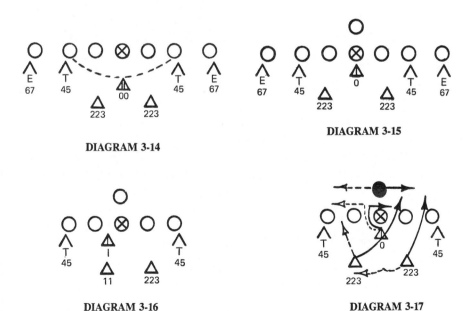

DIAGRAM 3-14

DIAGRAM 3-15

DIAGRAM 3-16

DIAGRAM 3-17

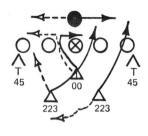

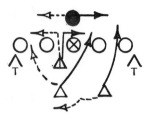

DIAGRAM 3-18   DIAGRAM 3-19

In the huddle, the signal caller says, "Fifty Bubble to Fifty Gap Stack Lucky-Blast Lucky." This means the defenders all line up as shown in Diagram 3-18.

THE CHANGING DEFENSIVE LOOKS

We want to keep our defensive look continually changing in the eyes of the offensive quarterback. Therefore we will use both a seven- and eight-man front, while incorporating the man-to-man, zone, and a combination of these two in our secondary pass defense. These defensive fronts must have the ability to successfully rush the passer and contain and force the offensive running attack. Thus, our basic defenses must have the ability to stunt, blitz, and jump the defenses to give the quarterback a variety of pre-snap reads.

WHEN TO VERBALIZE THE STEMS

At times we predetermine the defensive stunt, depending upon the offensive players' alignment. At other times our defensive signal-calling linebacker calls the stem just as the quarterback places his hands under the center. Generally we have one signal caller call the stem after a particular oral call or on a time count from the time the quarterback places his hands under the center. This time count, as previously mentioned, is determined by the scouting report's timing. There are some times when we will verbalize the stem predicated upon the motion of a particular offensive back.

Fifty Monster Slant Defense

While the Fifty Monster Defense looks strong to the side of the monster man, it is in reality strongest to the side of the slant, which is normally called away from the monster. In Diagram 4-1, the Responsibility Chart gives the viewer a concise look at the Fifty Monster Slant Defense, featuring the original alignment loops (rip technique) and slants and each of the front seven defender's responsibilities.

WHAT IS THE MONSTER DEFENSE?

The Monster Defense is a basic Oklahoma 5-4 defense with a three-deep secondary. This leaves another man, the monster man, who has the opportunity to declare himself:

1. To the wide side of the field.
2. Toward the strong side of the defense.
3. To the side emphasized in the scouting report, if the ball is in the middle of the field versus a balanced formation.

THE FIFTY MONSTER SLANT PRESSURE

The Fifty Monster Slant puts defensive pressure on the offensive attack. Football is a pressure game, and if the defense can pressure the offense into committing a handful of major mistakes, the offense will not be able to put together a long sustained march. This defense maximizes the chance that this pressure will force the offense into turnover on a fumble or interception. The forcing unit of the slant, scrape-off, or loop

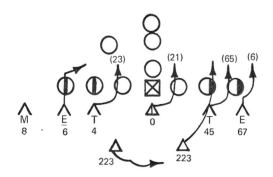

DIAGRAM 4-1a

FIFTY MONSTER SLANT DEFENSE RESPONSIBILITY CHART

	ALIGNMENT	MOVE TO	RESPONSIBILITIES
STRONG END	6	Ball	Contain-Pursue
WEAK END	67	8	Rip Ball
STRONG TACKLE	4	Rip 23	Penetrate — Ball
WEAK TACKLE	45	Rip 65	Penetrate — Ball
GUARD	0	Rip 21	Penetrate — Ball
SHUFFLE LINEBACKER	223	Shuffle	Scallop to Ball
SCRAPE LINEBACKER	223	Scrape 45	Blitz to Ball

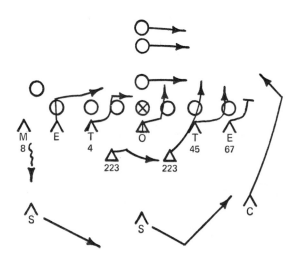

DIAGRAM 4-1b

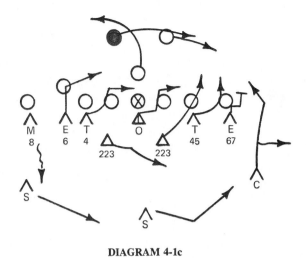

DIAGRAM 4-1c

techniques often causes the offense to miss an offensive blocking assignment, commit a penalty, or rattle the quarterback and make him call a poor play.

RIP TECHNIQUE

At times we want the defender to begin a loop and just skin or rip by the offensive blocker. Thus, we refer to this defensive technique as a "rip move." This differs from the loop technique, because the looping defender loops into a gap. The rip technique teaches the defender to take a short lead step, a crossover step, with the back foot, and then the defender rips his forearm flipper up and through the offensive player's inside shoulder pad (Diagram 4-2). Therefore, the rip defender is coached to fight outside blocking pressure by shuffling for as much width as possible. If no outside pressure shows, the rip defender is coached to close

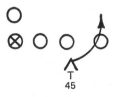

DIAGRAM 4-2
Rip Technique

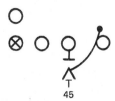

DIAGRAM 4-3

back toward the inside, keeping his shoulders parallel to the line of scrimmage. If the blocker attempts to block the rip defender one on one, the rip man is taught to hold his ground and fight pressure against the defender with his inside shoulder and forearm (Diagram 4-3).

If the defensive tackle has a rip technique on and the offensive blocker blocks away, the defender must be ready to take the proper pursuit angle to cut off the ball carrier. In this case, the defender is coached to flatten down his pursuit angle as both the key blocker and the ball go away (Diagram 4-4).

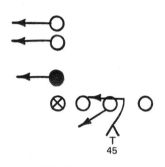

DIAGRAM 4-4

THE SLANTING MONSTER DEFENSE

We like to use the slant technique because it creates difficult blocking assignments for the offense and helps our defenders to penetrate into the backfield and often throws the opponent for a loss. It also forces many offensive mistakes and gives the normal Monster Defense a forcing facet. The slanting technique helps balance the defense away from the monster and in a direction many of our opponents choose to run. This defense also allows us to surprise the offensive blockers by blitzing (scraping) a linebacker, but only to the side of the flow of the ball. The defensive line's slants and loops also protect the linebackers from being blocked by the offense.

Actually, the defense shifts from a regular Fifty Odd alignment to an even "62" defensive look (Diagram 4-5). Thus, the defense has the opportunity to adjust a stunt to stop an over-shifted offensive formation.

When the ball goes away from the slant and toward the monster, the looping tackle, slanting tackle, slanting middle guard, and looping weak end must regroup and reverse their directions and pursue the ball carrier.

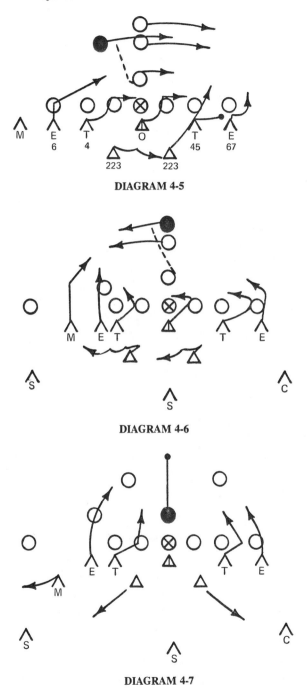

DIAGRAM 4-5

DIAGRAM 4-6

DIAGRAM 4-7

All are coached to take flat pursuit courses to get back and intercept the ball. The linebackers take a quick step in the slant direction and then scallop toward the ball (Diagram 4-6).

If a pass shows, all five linemen rush the passer in the correct channels; as illustrated in Diagram 4-7, the two linebackers drop back to defend the hook zones and the monster man covers his flat assignment. The three deep backs are locked into their deep coverage pattern (Diagram 4-7).

MONSTER DEFENSE'S ADVANTAGES

The Monster Defense protects the wide side of the field, placing an extra man (monster man) to the wide side. Since the ball is placed on or near the hash mark, about three-quarters of all plays and the opposition's runs to the wide side over three-quarters of the time, the offense ends up continually running into the Monster side of the defense.

The monster man is the only man who has to make a defensive adjustment to the opposition's offense to the wide side of the field.

Many offensive attacks will try to change their offensive attack away from the monster man, and that forces the opposition to run into the sidelines. We think of the sidelines as an extra defensive player; therefore, the offensive choice of plays has been limited.

When the football is directly in the middle of the field and the opposition has a tendency to run away from the monster man, we like to automatic a slant, some loop, or some other defensive stunt away from the monster. Thus, the offensive attack is directing their play situation into the most powerful force of the defensive front. This means that the defensive stunt away from the monster helps to compensate for the overshifted defense.

The monster man's position helps to simplify the Fifty defensive pass call, as the defense can play a straight three-deep locked-in pass defense opposed to the more difficult rotating box or corner defense. This means the monster will only have flat coverage on all passes, and only one man is responsible to cover the deep middle zone (safetyman).

The Monster game plan calls for the end to the side of the monster to always contain against a sprint-out pass. This also does away with the monster side tackle contain rush on pass plays, which is often a difficult assignment for some defensive Fifty tackles.

Whenever the ball is near the middle of the field, the monster man is taught to declare himself at the last moment. This means we often force the offense into calling a new play or at least a new direction on the line of scrimmage. This means our Monster Defense is forcing the offensive quarterback to play our game or make an offensive adjustment to our Monster Defense, and our defense can get zeroed in on the opposition's offensive plan of strategy.

The stunting or looping charge away from the monster helps to balance up our defense versus the triple optioning offensive attacks. The slants, loops, and other stunts away from the monster make the Monster Defense a difficult one for the triple-optioning blocking linemen to block.

THE MONSTER ASSIGNMENT AND RESPONSIBILITIES

On every play, prior to the snap, the monster must declare on which side of the offensive formation he will align himself. Basically, the monster is a contain man. If the play comes his way, the monster must close down the opening between himself and the defensive end so the offensive ball carrier cannot find the opening that may open up the offensive funnel. This means the monster's assignment is to force-contain or squeeze the ball carrier to the inside to give the defensive pursuit a chance to attack the ball carrier. If there is any question for the monster man when a sweep comes his way, the defender is coached to hang on the line of scrimmage to make sure the ball carrier stays to the monster's inside.

On the snap of the ball, the monster is coached to take a set step with the inside foot, and he is then taught to recognize the path of the ball. If the ball comes his way, he is coached to use his contain squeeze technique; if the play goes away, he is coached to cushion by dropping straight backward to reach a position so he can take his proper pursuit course. If the ball drops straight back (drop-back pass), the monster man is told to drop off the line into the flat to defend against the potential pass play. The monster is taught to hang on the line until he determines whether the quarterback is sprinting out back off the line of scrimmage or a deep sweep is developing, or if the quarterback is sprinting shallow (on the line of scrimmage) down the line.

STRONG END'S "6" ASSIGNMENTS AND RESPONSIBILITIES (MONSTER SIDE)

The strong end lines up about one foot off the line and head up on the offensive tight end. The defender is coached to keep the offensive tight end off the defensive tackle. The "6" defender can accomplish this task with his inside forearm or with his two-hand shiver. The defender is coached not to let the offensive end close down to his inside. This means the defensive end steps up inside with the inside foot and follows with a shuffle step with the backside foot. Thus, the defender is closing down to the inside, maintaining his shoulders square to the line of scrimmage.

The reason why this end is referred to as the strong end is that he is coached to anchor his position whenever a play comes his way. On a sweep, the defensive end must work his way laterally to the outside to minimize the open between the monster man and the strong end. If the play goes away, the defender is taught to trail the play, looking for any type of counter play coming back his way.

The strong end is always on the side of the monster; therefore, he rushes the passer from a containing outside-in angle on all types of passes. The only exception to the contain rush assignment for the strong end is when an X-stunt is called. When this stunt is called, the monster man exchanges his assignment with the defensive end, which calls for the monster man to contain rush on all pass plays. This means the monster is taught to take over all of the defensive anchor end's technique responsibilities. The strong end now picks up the defensive end's techniques and plays pass defense in the flat when the pass shows and cushions when play goes away from the strong end. If a sweep comes to the monster's side, the strong end must squeeze and contain just as the monster man does on his regular Fifty Defense (Diagram 4-8).

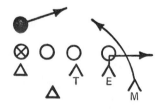

DIAGRAM 4-8

THE WEAK END'S "67" ALIGNMENT AND RESPONSIBILITIES (AWAY FROM MONSTER)

The weak end is the defensive end away from the monster man. He lines up in his normal "67" alignment, crowding the line of scrimmage.

His inside foot should be forward, splitting the outside leg of the offensive end. The weak end must contain the sweep, as he does not have the monster to his side. If the play comes his way as on a sprint-out pass, the defender must attack the quarterback from his outside-in angle. If play goes directly backward as in a drop-back pass, the weak end should drop off into the flat if a regular Fifty Defense has been called. If an option play comes his way, he is normally responsible to tackle the defensive quarterback. If the play goes off tackle, the defensive end must hang on the line of scrimmage until the weak end is sure that the ball carrier will not fake off tackle and then try to turn the corner as on a sweeping maneuver.

The defensive weak side end uses the same technique versus the offensive end, who closes down to the inside as previously explained in the description of the strong end.

THE VEER TACKLE'S "4" ALIGNMENT AND TECHNIQUES (STRONG SIDE TACKLE)

The veer tackle is lined up on the monster's side of the defensive line. He lines up in a "4" alignment which is head up on the offensive tackle. As soon as the ball is snapped, the veer tackle is coached to rip down over the offensive guard's outside shoulder ("23" area). The tackle is taught to close down on a 45 degree angle, stepping first with the inside foot and then crossing over with the outside foot. As soon as the defender uses his crossover step, he is coached to swing through his outside arm to protect against a possible cut-off block by the offensive tackle.

If the play is a quick maneuver toward the veer tackle, he must be prepared to meet the ball carrier with his shoulders squared to the line of scrimmage at the point of attack. It is planned that the defensive tackle's penetration off the slant will help to stunt the defender into the offensive backfield, affecting the timing of the offensive maneuver.

If the offensive guard tries to turn out on the slanting defender, the defensive tackle must continue to slant through the head of the guard to close down to the inside.

When the offensive guard blocks down on the middle guard, the veer tackle levels off and looks for the trap play. If a trap shows, the slant tackle must meet the trapper with his inside shoulder, keeping both shoulders square and stepping into the trapper with his inside foot and delivering a forearm with the inside shoulder in a quick one-two cadence. This means the veering tackle is taught to level off and close down the line to meet the trapper and minimize the potential trap hole.

If the offensive guard pulls either to his right or his left, the veering defender is coached to read the pulling route and follow the guard's path, which normally takes the veer tackle to the ball.

If the guard sets up to protect for a pass, the defensive tackle must rush, staying in his proper rush lane.

If the ball goes away, the veer tackle must close down through the guard-center gap, check for a possible counter play, and then set his proper pursuit course to intercept the ball carrier.

THE LOOP TACKLE'S "45" ALIGNMENT AND RESPONSIBILITIES (AWAY FROM MONSTER)

The tackle away from the monster is the loop tackle. He lines up in his normal "45" alignment and off the line of scrimmage. At the snap, the loop tackle takes a quick step laterally with his outside foot and looks at the offensive end. This loop technique is directed not for depth into the opposition's backfield, but to attack the position previously occupied by the tight end.

If the end does not block the looping tackle, he is coached to check for a block by the offensive tackle.

When the tight end blocks down on the looping defender, the defensive man meets the offensive end head up with his shoulders squared. The loop tackle is taught to play off the end with his hands and fight the blocker's pressure until the defender can determine the ball carrier's point of attack.

Any time the play goes away from the loop tackle, the defensive tackle is coached to be the Fifty Defense's trailing defender.

If neither the offensive end nor tackle attempts to block the looper, he looks to the inside and checks for a trapper taking an inside-out trap angle on the loop tackle's position.

Whenever a straight drop-back pass shows, the loop tackle is coached to take a contain route to rush the passer. The rushing defender is taught to keep the passer inside the pocket.

MIDDLE GUARD "0" ALIGNMENT AND RESPONSIBILITIES

The "0" defender is coached to crowd the center and line up on the pivot man's nose. On the snap of the ball, the middle guard slants away from the monster on a 45 degree angle, aiming at the outside hip of the offensive guard. As the middle guard begins his slant, he is taught to key the guard's movement.

If the guard blocks out on the slanting "0" man, he is coached to drive directly through the guard's head. If the ball carrier has already broken at an angle past the offensive guard, the defender is coached to spin out against the blocker's pressure and take a pursuit course to intercept the ball carrier.

The slant man must take a quick lead step with his slant side foot and then take a short crossover step with the back foot. The crossover step must be short, because the "0" defender must key the offensive guard for a possible pull to the right or the left. This means the middle guard must be ready to change directions quickly and get into the pulling guard's pocket, regardless of which direction the offensive man goes. This will bring the defender toward the point of the offensive attack.

Once the middle guard begins to slant and the offensive center tries to cut off the defender and the ball carrier goes away from the slant, the "0" defender must fight his way back; he must flatten out and take the proper pursuit course. Fighting against the center's cut-off block necessitates the use of the hands by the defender.

If a pass shows, the defensive middle guard must rush the passer, keeping an equidistant route between the slant and the loop tackles. The middle guard may use any one of his defensive rush techniques on the pass blockers, as long as he remains on his proper rush route.

SCRAPE LINEBACKER'S "223" ALIGNMENT AND RESPONSIBILITIES (AWAY FROM MONSTER)

The linebacker away from the monster's side is referred to as the scrape linebacker. He lines up in his normal "223" alignment, and his feet are lined up parallel to the line. The defender keys the ball and moves in that direction. His assignment is to scrape off behind the loop tackle's path. He is coached to scrape through to attack the play behind the line of scrimmage. The linebacker's first point of attack is off the shoulder of the offensive tackle's original alignment. That is the "45" area.

It is most difficult for the scrape linebacker to determine where the ball is when the flow of most of the backs goes one way and the ball goes the other direction in a counter type maneuver. When this happens, the defender must take a set step in his scrape-off direction, but has to locate the ball before over-committing which might take the "223" defender completely out of the play.

When the ball goes away from the scrape backer, he must take his normal pursuit course and scallop for the ball carrier regardless of any threat of the counter play.

If a back-up pass develops, the scrape backer drops back to his regular hook zone. He is coached to sprint backward on a 45 degree angle, looking for the tight end's pass pattern course. If the tight end runs straight forward, the scrape linebacker is taught to get in front of the end and take away his straight course by chugging the potential receiver with a two-hand shiver. The defender must make sure the ball is not in flight when he shivers the tight end. Then the linebacker is coached to level off about ten yards deep and look at the passer. The backer is coached to go for the ball on the movement of the passer's forward arm. He is in an excellent position to make the interception, as long as he takes a chance to cut in front of the hooking receiver. If no man hooks in his assigned defensive area, the scrape linebacker is coached to slide outside to protect the deeper and wider curl zone.

If the quarterback sprints out his way on a potential sprint-out or roll-out pass, the defender is assigned to scrape off through his normal assigned "45" area and rush the passer (Diagram 4-9).

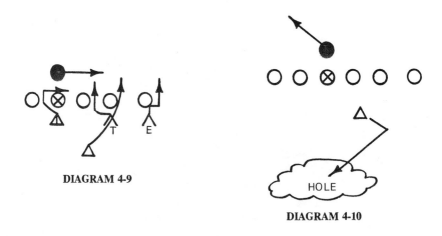

DIAGRAM 4-9

HOLE

DIAGRAM 4-10

When the quarterback sprints out away, the linebacker is coached to begin to drop back into his hook area and then sprint for the "hole." The "hole" is a deep middle area directly in front of the center's original position. The "hole" area moves in the direction of the sprint-out passer as the passer moves toward the sidelines. The scrape linebacker must take this deep vacated area to look for any possible throw-back pass (Diagram 4-10).

SHUFFLE LINEBACKER'S TECHNIQUES

The shuffle linebacker lines up in his normal "223" alignment to the side of the monster back. The linebacker's key is the near offensive back through the head of the offensive guard. His defensive responsibilities and techniques are the same as those of the normal Fifty Oklahoma linebacker. He keys first the blocking path of his offensive guard.

If the offensive guard attempts to reach block on the linebacker, he picks up the direction of the near side back. The defender must get rid of the blocking offensive guard and then focus his entire attention on the near back and the direction of the near back. The "223" defender is taught to scallop along the line of scrimmage, checking each hole for a possible point of attack (Diagram 4-11). The defender must stay on the ball carrier's backside hip so he will not overrun the ball carrier. Staying on the backside hip of the ball carrier enables the linebacker to square off his shoulders to the line of scrimmage as soon as the ball carrier turns up toward the line of scrimmage. The defender is coached to step up and meet the ball carrier head on (Diagram 4-12).

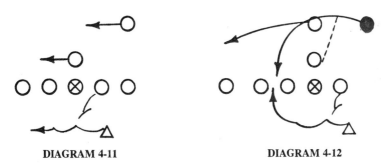

DIAGRAM 4-11   DIAGRAM 4-12

When the near guard blocks the shuffle linebacker head on, the "223" defender must deliver a forearm blow on the blocking offensive guard, get rid of the potential blocker, and then step up and take on the near offensive back. If the near back is the ball carrier on a quick dive

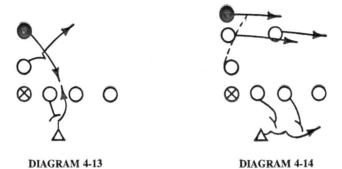

DIAGRAM 4-13   DIAGRAM 4-14

play, the linebacker must remain in a good position, keeping his shoulders parallel to the line of scrimmage, and tackle the dive man. The shuffle linebacker must keep his outside arm free to ward off a block from his outside (Diagram 4-13).

When the offensive guard attempts to reach on the linebacker and the near back runs a route to the linebacker's outside, the defender must be ready for a reach comeback block from the offensive tackle or a down block from the offensive tight end. Therefore, the scalloping defender must keep his outside arm free to ward off any possible outside blocker as he shuffles to the outside with his shoulders parallel to the line of scrimmage (Diagram 4-14).

If the quarterback drops straight back for a pocket pass or sprints out to the shuffle linebacker's side, the defender is coached to drop back on a 45 degree angle to his hook zone. As he drops back, he looks for any possible offensive receiver running straight downfield toward the hook zone. Once the shuffle linebacker sees the tight end, slot, or near back running this type of route, the defender is taught to chug the receiver. The coaching point behind this defensive chug technique is for the linebacker to look up the near receivers to his side as soon as pass shows. He keeps his eyes on the receiver until he makes contact with the potential receiver, and then the backer levels off at ten to twelve yards and plays his hook zone. If no one comes into his zone, the defender is coached to slide further outside and defend the curl zone (Diagram 4-15).

When the quarterback sprints out for a pass away from the shuffle linebacker, the defender starts for his normal hook zone, but reverses his direction and drops back toward the deep hole area as the quarterback continues to drop back on his sprint-out angle. This is the same technique

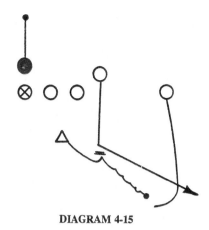

DIAGRAM 4-15

that is used by the scrape linebacker whenever a sprint-out pass goes away
from the scraper's position.

PLAY IT STRAIGHT VS. FLIP-FLOP DEFENSE

The merit of playing a flip-flop defense is that one side of your
defense will always be to the wide side of the field because the offense
usually runs to that side of the field. The flip-flop defense may also go to
the strength of the offensive formation for the same reason whenever the
ball is near the middle of the field. Naturally, the strongest defenders
would be stationed to the wide side of the field or to the power side of the
opponent's formation.

The advantages of playing a straight defense (the right side defender
always plays the right side regardless of field position or the strength of
the offensive formation) is that the defender uses only one major forearm
blow. He always plays to the same side of the field and he only has to
practice defending one side of the defense. He does not have to alter his
stance or his defensive techniques at the last moment, depending on how
the power side of the offense lines up. Therefore, the primary advantage
of the straight defense is the defender only practices playing on one
particular side of the defense, using the same stance and forearm in all
practice sessions and games.

Another argument against flip-flopping is that we want to know right
now, if the offense begins to sweep or run off tackle to our right side,
what defenders are responsible for the offensive gains. If the flip-flop

technique is employed, it is difficult for some of the coaches (especially down on the field) to know if the offensive formation was right or left, etc.

Yet we still refer to our strong end or strong tackle as long as these defenders are on the strong side of the defense. As soon as they are aligned on the weak side, they automatically become the weakside end or weakside tackle, respectively.

How to Coach the Fifty
Monster Slant Techniques

The reader may find the over-all picture of the Fifty Monster Slant Defense and the exact techniques and stunting responsibilities in Diagram 4-1 in Chapter 4.

This present chapter features the individual slants of the seven-man defensive front illustrated in diagrams and explained in written technical coaching points.

MIDDLE GUARD'S ANGLE TECHNIQUES

The middle guard is coached to key the movement of the ball. He is coached to slant toward the offensive guard, executing a 45 degree angle with the near foot lead step. The middle guard is coached to read the offensive guard on his first step; if the guard attempts to block the slanting defender, the middle guard is taught to step with the backside foot and bring up the outside arm. The defender must stay low and penetrate, driving through the offensive guard's inside hip. This is a rip move, ripping through the guard's outside hip. The defender must square his shoulders parallel to the line of scrimmage so he can flatten his course shallow back toward the center if the ball goes away from the veer technique (Diagram 5-1).

If the center attempts to cut off the middle guard, the defender *must* use his arms to ward off the potential blocker, keeping the elbows locked. The middle guard should attempt to jam the center's head down so he can maneuver around the center's cut-off block. The middle guard must

DIAGRAM 5-1   **DIAGRAM 5-2**

swing his backside foot around quickly so that the nose defender will end up with his shoulders parallel to the line of scrimmage (Diagram 5-2).

When the center and guard attempt to double team the middle defender, he is coached to stay low and attempt to fight pressure of the outside blockers and possibly split the double team block. He must fight pressure and read as a last resort; when trapped, he is taught to whirl or spin out shallow and pursue the ball carrier (Diagram 5-3).

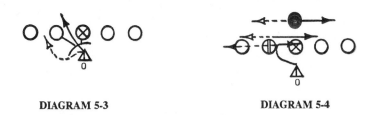

DIAGRAM 5-3   **DIAGRAM 5-4**

If a pass shows, the middle guard must attack and get his shoulders square to the line and then rush the passer. He must stay equidistant between the two defensive tackles when rushing the sprint-out pass toward the slant, back-up pass, or sprint out away from the middle guard's slant (Diagram 5-4).

Whenever the slanting middle guard reads the guard pulling, the defender is coached to get into the pulling guard's pocket and then pursue the ball carrier. This means the middle guard must flatten out in a hurry when the guard pulls toward the center, driving off his outside foot and dipping the inside shoulder. If the guard pulls away, the defender must push off the inside foot (after squaring his shoulders), and dip his outside shoulder and flatten to follow the hip of the pulling guard (Diagram 5-5).

The most important coaching point pertaining to the middle guard's slant technique is that he must protect his slant area and never get cut off from his assigned area.

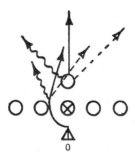

DIAGRAM 5-5

VEER TACKLE'S TECHNIQUES

The veer tackle is coached to line up in his "4" alignment head up on the offensive tackle. He moves on the movement of the hand of the offensive tackle. The "4" defender must look for a possible block from the offensive tackle and then pick up the offensive guard's read after the veer tackle makes his first step. The veer target is to rip through the outside shoulder of the guard and penetrate with the shoulders squared to the line of scrimmage. The veer tackle is taught to stay low and make his body small, so he can squeeze between the blockers. It is most important that the defender's feet are perpendicular to the line of scrimmage and that he penetrates only to the depth of the offensive linemen's original position. The exception to the rule is when pass shows and the tackle must rush the passer.

If the offensive tackle blocks one on one directly on the defender, there is no definite read for the veer tackle. Thus, the defender must run his rip charge, taking on the main blocker and then locating the football (Diagram 5-6). The "4" alignment should minimize the offensive blocker's angle on the veering defender.

DIAGRAM 5-6   **DIAGRAM 5-7**

When the offensive guard attempts to block out on the veer tackle, the defender must beat him, fighting through the head of the offensive guard. If the offensive guard does get the angle on the veer defender, he must go straight through the blocker's head. The "4" alignment should minimize this offensive blocking angle (Diagram 5-7).

When the ball carrier runs toward the veer tackle's side, both the offensive guard and the offensive tackle will try to reach block. As soon as the veer tackle begins his slant technique, he must read the reach block and fight its pressure. The offensive tackle may reach, then hold to just off the defensive tackle. At times it is best for the veer tackle to go under the reach-pick block if he has time to cut off the ball carrier (Diagram 5-8).

DIAGRAM 5-8   DIAGRAM 5-9

If the offense uses a turn-out block by the guard and a fold block by the tackle, the veer tackle is coached to attack the guard's block, as in Diagram 5-9. As a last resort, the defensive tackle may have to spin out (Diagram 5-9). The defender is cautioned to spin out as shallow as possible and always opposite the pressure of the offensive block.

Against a trap play, the veer tackle is coached to run his slant technique and to close to the inside if not blocked. Whenever the defensive tackle is not blocked, he must look to the inside for a trap play and maintain his shoulders parallel to the line of scrimmage as he closes down and looks for the trap play. Normally, the offensive guard will block down to pick up the middle guard, and the offensive tackle will normally loop down and attempt to pick off the inside Fifty linebacker (Diagram 5-10).

The veer tackle reacts to the double team block in the same manner as he fights off the one-on-one block.

Rushing the drop-back passer, the veer tackle rushes over the "23" area and puts on an all-out rush. He must make a check for a possible draw, but this read is on the run (Diagram 5-11). If the quarterback sprints out in either direction, the defender is taught to flatten out his course and

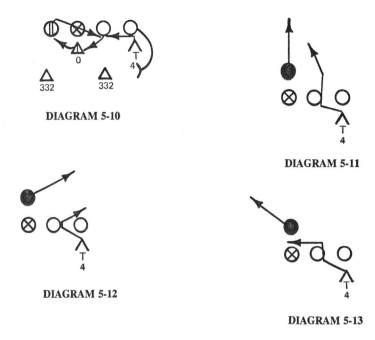

DIAGRAM 5-10

DIAGRAM 5-11

DIAGRAM 5-12

DIAGRAM 5-13

pursue down the line to the outside versus a sprint out toward the veer tackle's original position (Diagram 5-12). As soon as the passer sprints out away from the veer tackle's original position, the veering defender again flattens out his course, only this time, he flattens out his pursuit-rush course away from his original aligned position (Diagram 5-13). The veer tackle must defend against the draw play to his side.

LOOP TACKLE'S TECHNIQUES

The loop tackle lines up in his "4" alignment and loops exactly over the inside hip of the tight end's original position. This is referred to by our defensive coaches as a rip technique, as the defender rips up and through the tight end's inside hip.

As soon as the offensive tackle moves his hand, the loop tackle begins his loop toward the defensive "65" area. If the offensive tackle attempts to hook the looping defensive tackle, the defender should fight through and beyond the tackle reach block. As soon as the loop tackle reaches his "65" area, he must keep his outside arm free and flatten out away from the offensive end's hook block, so the defender will be able to

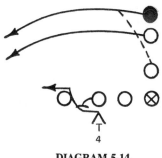

DIAGRAM 5-14

take a proper pursuit angle to head off the ball carrier (Diagram 5-14). The defensive loop tackle does not have any read; he can only defeat the hook block to the outside.

Against the turn-out block by the tackle, the loop defender must execute his loop technique, then level off, flatten out, and take a flat pursuit course down the line toward the offensive center and the ball carrier (Diagram 5-15).

DIAGRAM 5-15   **DIAGRAM 5-16**

The loop tackle defends against the double team block the same way he does versus the drive block by the offensive tight end. The looping defender steps toward the offensive end and reads the offensive end's first step. As soon as the "4" defender reads the tight end drive route, he is coached to explode into the down blocking end with his outside forearm. This is the same technique that is used against the tight end's single or double blocking technique (Diagram 5-16).

If no offensive blocker blocks, it may be the trap play or Triple Option. Whenever we face a Triple Optioning team, we normally coach our defender to tackle the quarterback; but, of course, we have several exceptions to this general rule. If we are not facing a Triple Option attack, the first thing the loop tackle looks for is an inside-out trap by a pulling offensive trapper. The defender must close down as quickly as possible and keep his shoulders square to the line of scrimmage as he begins to close. The defender must not penetrate, but must maintain a flat course shallow to the line of scrimmage. The defender is coached to take on the trapper with the inside foot and the inside shoulder and forearm. He should close down as far as possible to minimize the size of the trap hole (Diagram 5-17).

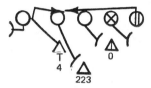

DIAGRAM 5-17

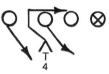

DIAGRAM 5-18

When the ball goes away from the loop tackle, he is coached to pursue the ball just a yard less than the depth of the ball. The reason we want the pursuing loop tackle to pursue a yard less than the depth of the ball is so the defender will not overpursue and get blocked out on any type of offensive counter plays (Diagram 5-18).

This means that against the ground attack, the loop tackle must stop the one-on-one and double team attack and close off the off-tackle hole. He must close off the trap hole and reach from an outside-in angle on all quick offensive dive plays. When the ball goes away, the defensive tackle must chase the ball, because the defensive end away from the monster must be ready to drop off into the flat and defend against the pass.

Against the pass, the loop tackle must rush the passer in the same manner as the veer tackle's pass rush technique. See Diagrams 5-11, 5-12, and 5-13.

THE STRONG SIDE END'S TECHNIQUES

The defensive strong end lines up in his "6" technique and is coached to deliver a blow on the offensive end and anchor his defensive position.

If the defensive end blocks one on one versus the strong end, the defender is coached to use a forearm or two-hand shiver on the tight end. The defensive end anchors his position first, fights pressure, gets rid of the blocker, and then pursues (Diagram 5-19).

When the offensive end tries to hook the strong end, the defender is coached to get to the outside, fighting through the head of the hooking

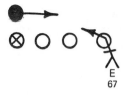

DIAGRAM 5-19

blocker. The strong end should look for some type of quick sweep. The defender should attempt to stretch out the sweep, because the monster to his side has his squeeze contain assignment (Diagram 5-20). The defensive end should work to his outside to cut down the opening between the monster and the strong end.

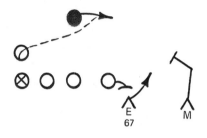

DIAGRAM 5-20

As the offensive end blocks down, the defensive end must deliver a blow on the tight end and close down with him and fight to keep the down-blocking end off the inside linebackers. Then the defender is taught to close down to the inside and attack the off-tackle hole from his outside-in angle (Diagram 5-21).

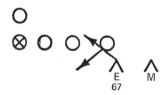

DIAGRAM 5-21

As soon as any type of pass shows, the strong end is coached to rush the passer. He must rush from the outside-in and contain any possible scramble technique his way by the quarterback (Diagram 5-22).

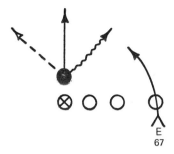

DIAGRAM 5-22

THE WEAK END'S TECHNIQUES

The end away from the monster, commonly referred to as the weak end, lines up in his normal "67" alignment. He is responsible for the outside contain area. He must be quick against the offensive running plays and must be agile enough to drop off into the flat to play pass defense.

He must play a technique similar to that used by the defensive strong end against the run when a tight end is on his side. When the split end shows to his side, we often give the defender the option of remaining on the line of scrimmage or adjusting his position slightly off the line of scrimmage. The weak end now must be cognizant of the fact that he is more susceptible to a crack back block by the split end.

The defensive weak end must be ready for a crack block from the split end. The deep defensive back to the weak end's side should yell "Crack-crack!" This should alert the defender of the crack back block. Once the sweep begins, the defensive end makes a quick head and shoul-

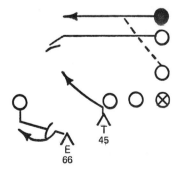

DIAGRAM 5-23

der fake to the inside to fake out the cracking split end. After the quick fake has been made, the end should then step back and lose ground to get to the outside and gain leverage on the sweeping ball carrier (Diagram 5-23).

DEFENSIVE WEAK END PASS DEFENSE (AWAY FROM MONSTER)

Away from the monster, the defensive end has pass coverage responsibilities whenever the quarterback uses his back-up pass or sprints out. On both of these occasions, the defensive end drops back on his outside foot and picks up any potential receiver who may attempt to run into the flat area (Diagram 5-24).

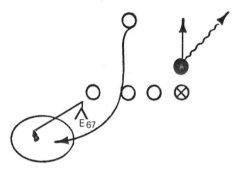

DIAGRAM 5-24

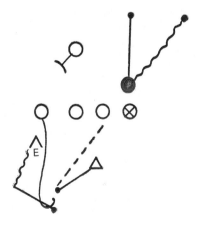

DIAGRAM 5-25

Once the defensive end drops off into the flat, he looks up any receiver who breaks into the flat. If a receiver enters his area, he is coached to let the receiver come to him. If the near back does not release, the defensive end reads the tight offensive end. If the end releases and hooks, the defender is taught to squeeze the hooking end from the outside-in, while the inside linebacker is attacking an inside-out angle. This means that both defenders will sandwich the receiver and take away the hook pattern (Diagram 5-25).

If the defensive end away from the monster is on the offensive split end's side, he keys the split end and looks for the quick slant or veer pass and takes away that pattern first, by going through the head of the potential slant receiver (Diagram 5-26).

If the split end attempts to run a sideline route, the defensive end

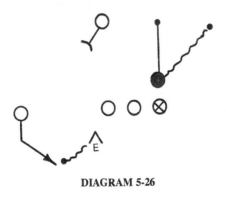

DIAGRAM 5-26

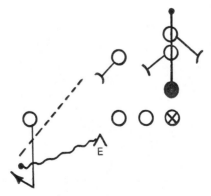

DIAGRAM 5-27

sprints for a point in between the passer and the area the end is sprinting for. This forces the passer to put an arc on the ball and gives the deep back a chance to recover and make a play on the pass. If the passer does not throw the ball high enough, the defensive end has the opportunity to pick the ball off in the flat, and it is clear sailing from this flat area (Diagram 5-27).

From the deep flat position illustrated in Diagram 5-27, the defensive end is in excellent position to pick up the near back if he attempts to run a delayed flare route behind the line of scrimmage (Diagram 5-28). When this happens, the defensive end attacks the flare end as soon as the quarterback puts the ball into the air. The defender must attack the flare end from an outside-in angle (Diagram 5-28).

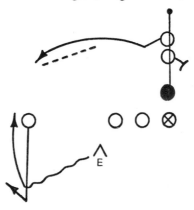

DIAGRAM 5-28

After sprinting to take away the sideline pass route of the split end, he may see the near back run a short flat course, and the defender must release from his sideline defensive pass assignment. Then he must attack the short flat pattern of the near back as demonstrated in Diagram 5-29. The defensive end is coached to go through the near back's outside shoulder for the possible interception. He must time his defensive contact so he is making a bonafide attempt to go for the ball. Using this pass defense technique makes it legal for the defender to make contact with the potential receiver, even if he cannot make the interception.

Whenever the quarterback sprints away from the defensive end to the split end's side and no back releases, he should key the split end all the way. This means the defender can cushion more because the sprint-away

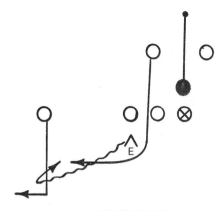

DIAGRAM 5-29

quarterback has to throw across his body to successfully complete the sideline pass. Now the defender is coached to look for the possible curl pass or some other inside route by the split end. If the curl pass shows, the defender must play this pass the same as illustrated in Diagram 5-30 versus the hook end's pass pattern. The cushioning defensive end should try to force the potential receiver to the inside toward the inside linebacker. We ask the defensive end to accelerate at the last moment and attempt to cross the face of the receiver for an interception if possible (Diagram 5-30).

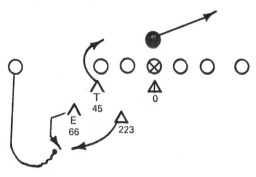

DIAGRAM 5-30

SCRAPE LINEBACKER'S TECHNIQUES (AWAY FROM MONSTER)

The scrape linebacker lines up in his normal "223" position about two and one-half yards off the line of scrimmage. As soon as the ball goes to his side, the scraper is coached to scrape through the original "45" defensive area and penetrate to attack the ball. Actually whenever the ball goes to the scrape linebacker's side, this linebacker becomes a blitzing linebacker. The "223" backer also attacks the quarterback whenever a sprint-out pass toward the scrape defender's side shows.

Against a sweep to the scraper's side, the scrape linebacker shoots over the loop tackle's vacated "45" area and attacks the sweep from his inside-out angle. The scrape linebacker must use his inside arm lift to help ward off any reaching blockers. The linebacker must keep his outside arm free to take on any potential outside blockers (Diagram 5-31).

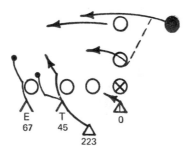

DIAGRAM 5-31

If the quarterback sprints out toward the scraper, the defensive linebacker scrapes through the "45" area and blitzes the quarterback in an all-out pass rush (Diagram 5-32).

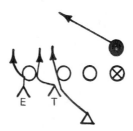

DIAGRAM 5-32

If the ball goes away, the scrape linebacker must take a set step in his normal scrape direction and then locate the ball. He first takes a picture of the play and checks for any comeback counter plays, and then plays a regular Fifty linebacker and scallops down the line to cut off the ball carrier. As he scallops, the linebacker is taught to check each hole for a

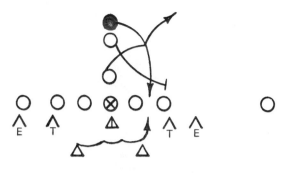

DIAGRAM 5-33

possible cut by the ball carrier (Diagram 5-33). As soon as the linebacker determines what hole the ball carrier will select, the defender must meet the ball carrier with his shoulders parallel to the line of scrimmage (Diagram 5-33).

When a drop-back pass or sprint-out pass play begins to develop, the Fifty linebacker must drop back to his hook zone (with a tight end to his side), and get into the path of the hooking end's pass route. If the tight end runs a straight hook cut, the defensive linebacker is coached to chug the offensive end, then level off at about ten to twelve yards deep and look for the quick pass by the quarterback. As soon as the quarterback sprints away, the scrape linebacker should begin to drop back to his normal hook zone on a 45 degree angle, looking for a possible pull-up

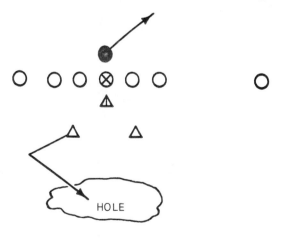

DIAGRAM 5-34

throw-back pass. If the quarterback continues to sprint out, the linebacker is taught to begin to move toward the sprint-out quarterback's direction on a 45 degree angle and go to the deep hole area over the middle of the defensive secondary (Diagram 5-34).

SHUFFLE LINEBACKER'S TECHNIQUES (TO MONSTER)

The shuffle linebacker also lines up in his normal "223" alignment. The linebacker's key is the ball and the near back. If the guard goes directly at the linebacker in a one-on-one blocking technique and the near back dives, the linebacker must meet the pressure of the blocker with a solid forearm blow and neutralize the blocker. Then he must get rid of the blocker and attack the diving ball carrier (Diagram 5-35).

DIAGRAM 5-35

What Are the Basic Fifty Bubble and Revert Defenses?

One of the newest and most popular variations of the Fifty Defense is the Fifty Bubble and Revert Defenses. Since many coaches wanted a more maneuverable middle guard, they moved him off the line of scrimmage; then the defense had only two down linemen and these were the two defensive tackles! The middle three linebackers, two to four yards depth off the line of scrimmage, created a large bubble-like look in the defense, hence the Bubble Defense (Diagram 6-1). The three-man Bubble

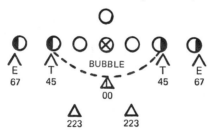

DIAGRAM 6-1

was used basically against two tight ends, and the Revert look came about when the defensive coaches wanted to revert to moving one of the linebackers in an adjusted "44" alignment to a split end side only. Thus, the Fifty Revert Defense came about as an adjustment to the split end offensive attacks (Diagram 6-2). The middle guard turned middle linebacker also added a pass defender versus the quick swing, circle, and

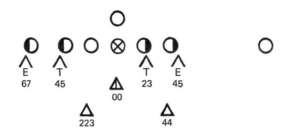

DIAGRAM 6-2

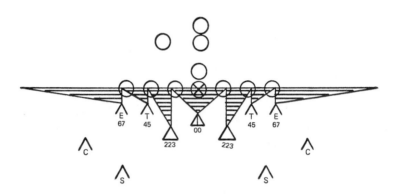

FIFTY BUBBLE RESPONSIBILITY CHART

	ALIGNMENT	KEYS BY PROGRESSION	RESPONSIBILITY
ENDS	67	(1) End (2) Near Back (3) Fullback	End to sidelines
TACKLES	45	(1) Tackle (2) End (3) Near Back	Tackle to nose of end
LINEBACKERS	223	Flow of backs Fast and slow reads	Step up and attack ball Nose of guard to tackle
MIDDLE LINEBACKERS	00	Flow of backs Fast and slow reads	Step up and attack ball Fast and slow reads Tackle to tackle

DIAGRAM 6-3a

loop pass routes of the fullback, as an extra receiver from a more spread or Pro offensive look.

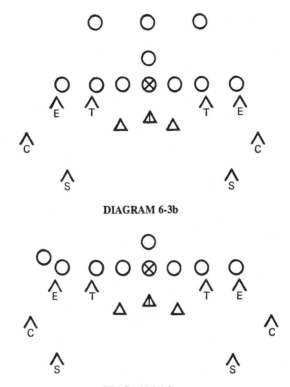

DIAGRAM 6-3b

DIAGRAM 6-3c

A clearer and more detailed view of both the Fifty Bubble and Fifty Revert Defenses may be found in Diagrams 6-3 and 6-4. These diagrams illustrate the Bubble and Revert Responsibility Charts. All of the defenders' positions are numbered in three diagrams and the defenders' progressive keys and responsibilities are shown in chart form.

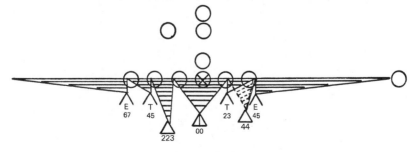

DIAGRAM 6-4a

<u>FIFTY REVERT RESPONSIBILITY CHART</u>

	ALIGNMENT	KEYS BY PROGRESSION	RESPONSIBILITY
ENDS	67	(1) End (2) Near Back (3) Fullback	End defender on the line to the sidelines
TACKLES	45	(1) Tackle (2) End (3) Near back	Tackle to nose of the end
FIFTY LINEBACKER	223	(1) Guard (2) Near back	Nose of guard to tackle
MIDDLE LINEBACKER	00	(1) Quarterback (2) Fullback (3) Near back	Guard to opposite guard
REVERT LINEBACKER	44	(1) Guard (2) Tackle (3) Near back	Guard to tackle

Diagram 6-4a (*continued*)

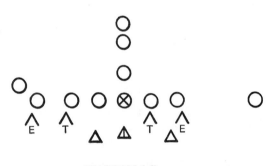

DIAGRAM 6-4b

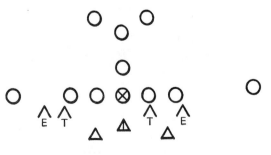

DIAGRAM 6-4c

THE FIFTY BUBBLE DEFENSE

The Bubble Defense resembles an Oklahoma or Fifty Defense, with all three linebackers in the middle forming a bubble-like look.

If the opposition employs a split end, the defensive signal caller may ask for a Revert call to the split end side. This moves the weakside or shortside linebacker over the offensive tackle on the split end's side "44." The defensive end lines up to the outside of the tackle in his normal "45" position. The defensive tackle moves into his position on the outside shoulder of the guard to the split end's side. The other defenders line up in their normal positions. This alignment is called a Fifty Revert Defense, a form of the Fifty Bubble Defense.

MIDDLE LINEBACKER ("00")

Alignment: He lines up head on the center. If too large a split exists between guard-center gap, he takes the gap in a four-point stance.

Stance: The linebacker should line up head on the center about two yards deep in a good two-point position with his feet in a parallel stance. His legs should be bent and ready to move in any direction. His arms should hang relaxed just inside his knees; his head should be up and his butt down. His body weight should be evenly distributed on the balls of his feet.

Key and Reaction: The linebacker should key the center's head and then the inside shoulder of the near back. The middle linebacker moves on movement and then reads the ball and the line's blocking pattern on the move.

Read: There are two basic reads, the quick read and the slow read. The quick read is when all of the backs go to one side or the other (Diagrams 6-5a, 6-5b, 6-5c, and 6-5d). If the near back dives directly at

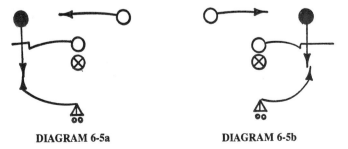

DIAGRAM 6-5a   DIAGRAM 6-5b

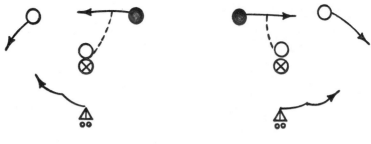

DIAGRAM 6-5c   DIAGRAM 6-5d

the middle linebacker, the linebacker must explode into the blocker, fight the pressure of the block by continually moving upfield, and attack the back at the point of attack (Diagrams 6-6a, 6-6b, 6-6c, 6-6d).

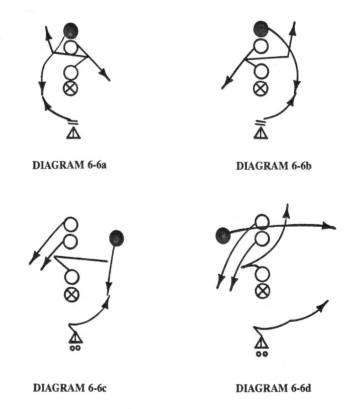

DIAGRAM 6-6a   DIAGRAM 6-6b

DIAGRAM 6-6c   DIAGRAM 6-6d

The slow read results when the backs go in opposite directions. Whenever the slow read takes place, the middle linebacker holds for a moment, then steps up, meets pressure, and next, locates the ball. The reason we use the slow read on crossing or misdirection by the offensive backs is to teach the defender to spin his wheels and not rush after fakes (Diagrams 6-6a, 6-6b, 6-6c, and 6-6d). This is called a slow read.

As soon as the center puts his hands on the ball, the middle linebacker should concentrate on his quarterback-fullback keys (Diagram 6-7). Once the ball has been put into play, the middle linebacker should read the center and both guards on the move (Diagram 6-8).

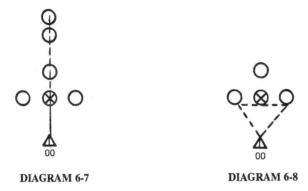

DIAGRAM 6-7   DIAGRAM 6-8

Coaching Note: Middle linebacker *keys* personnel on snap of the ball, then *reads* offensive blocking patterns on the run as he attacks the ball.

If the center blocks head up on the middle linebacker, he should use a two-arm shiver to be able to deliver a blow on the center's helmet or shoulders and fight the pressure of the center's block. The middle linebacker must be able to control the center and then disengage the blocker once the defender recognizes the direction of the ball. The middle linebacker must be drilled in delivering his two-arm shiver and not try to sneak a look at the ball carrier before he delivers his blow. As soon as the linebacker gets rid of or disengages the center, he must square his shoulders parallel to the line of scrimmage before he begins to pursue the flow of the ball (Diagram 6-9).

When the center blocks back on the defensive tackle to the split end side (Revert Call, Diagram 6-10), the middle linebacker must be ready to step up and look for the trap or isolation play. He is coached to step with the foot to the center's direction, find the ball, square his shoulders, and pursue the ball carrier. If the opposition attempts to run a sweep, the

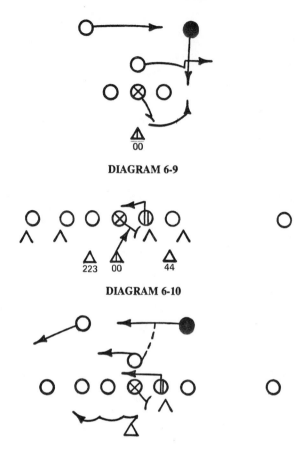

DIAGRAM 6-9

DIAGRAM 6-10

DIAGRAM 6-11

middle linebacker must step up to plug the trap area and then scallop to the outside to pursue the sweep (Diagram 6-11).

MIDDLE LINEBACKER'S RESPONSIBILITIES:

Key the center's head and the near back (Diagram 6-12).

Read the blocking pattern of the center and frontside guard (Diagram 6-13).

When the quarterback drops straight back for a pocket pass, the middle linebacker should drop back into the middle hook zone, favoring the strong side (tight end side) of the offensive formation (Diagram 6-14).

When the quarterback sprints or rolls out, breaking the guard box,

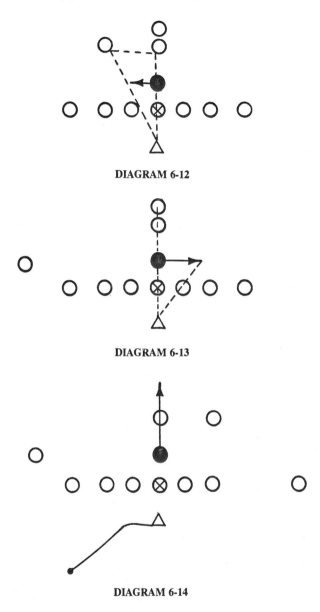

DIAGRAM 6-12

DIAGRAM 6-13

DIAGRAM 6-14

the middle linebacker should mirror the route and sprint for the hook zone to the side of the flow. If the tight end runs a hook pattern, the middle linebacker should collision him (Diagram 6-15). If the quarterback runs a sprint out to the split end side and the running back attempts to run a divide pattern down the seam, the middle linebacker should collision the running back and defend the hook or curl zone (Diagram 6-16).

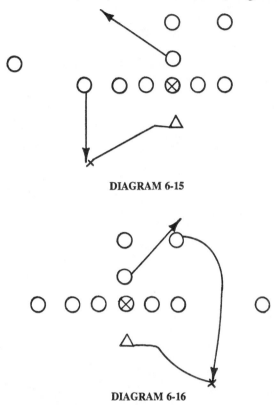

DIAGRAM 6-15

DIAGRAM 6-16

Coaching Points (Middle Linebacker):

1. Hang or spin your wheels on slow read, then attack the ball moving upfield.
2. Attack all sweeps and off-tackle plays from an inside-out angle.
3. You are responsible for all draw plays.
4. Key man for direction of movement.
5. Read the blocking pattern of the center and two guards on the move.
6. Play the run first and the pass second.
7. Sprint to strong side, take strong hook zone.
8. Sprint to weak side, check divide pass in the hook zone. If no one enters hook zone, slide to curl zone.

9. Adjust depth according to down, distance, formation, and game situations.
10. Knock down delayed dragging or crossing receiver with forearm blow.
11. Scallop to the outside on all off-tackle and sweeps, keeping the shoulders parallel to the line of scrimmage, and stay on the hip of the ball carrier. Don't overrun the ball carrier.
12. Get rid of the blocker as soon as possible.
13. Take the proper pursuit course with quickness and speed.
14. Gang tackling makes champions. The middle linebacker should be in on all tackles.
15. If you commit yourself to the run on a play action pass, continue through with the attack and rush the passer.
16. The middle linebacker must be a pressure guy both mentally and physically. He must be able to make the proper defensive call and be able to make the big play.

STRONG AND WEAK LINEBACKERS

Alignment: The strong linebacker lines up to the tight end side on the outside shoulder of the offensive guard (''223'' technique). If Bubble is called, the weak linebacker lines up in the same alignment over the split side offensive guard. If Revert is called, the weak linebacker lines up directly over the split side offensive tackle (''44'' technique), about three to four yards deep (Diagram 6-17).

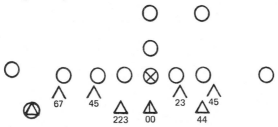

DIAGRAM 6-17

Stance: The linebacker should use a two-point football stance, using a good football position with his legs bent and ready to move in any direction. His arms should hang relaxed just inside his knees; his head should be up and his butt down. His body weight should be evenly distributed on the balls of his feet.

Key and Reaction: The strong linebacker ("223") should key the near back through the offensive guard. The weak linebacker should key the offensive tackle (Revert call).

Read: The strong side linebacker has two basic reads—the quick read and the slow read. The quick read for the inside strong linebacker is when one or all backs flow to the same side, toward him or away from the strong linebacker. The strong side linebacker lines up over the strong side offensive guard. If the near back dives directly at the strong side linebacker and the other backs flow in his direction, the linebacker is taught to explode into the blocker, fight pressure of the block, and then attack the ball carrier at the point of the attack. This is called the fast read (Diagrams 6-18a, 6-18b, 6-18c, 6-18d).

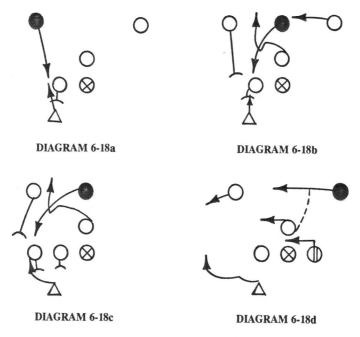

DIAGRAM 6-18a   DIAGRAM 6-18b

DIAGRAM 6-18c   DIAGRAM 6-18d

The second type of read for the strong side linebacker is the slow read. The slow read takes place when the backs go in opposite directions from each other. Whenever the slow read develops, the strong side linebacker is coached to spin his wheels by taking a picture of the backfield maneuver, then step up to meet pressure of the blocker and locate the ball. The reason we coach the slow read for the strong side linebacker, on crossing or misdirection maneuvers caused by the offensive backs, is to teach the defender to check who has the ball before he takes off rushing after a faking back. This is called a slow read (Diagrams 6-19a, 6-19b, 6-19c, and 6-19d).

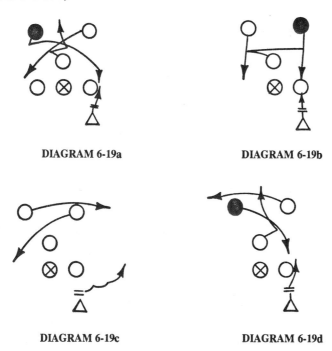

DIAGRAM 6-19a   DIAGRAM 6-19b

DIAGRAM 6-19c   DIAGRAM 6-19d

The weakside linebacker keys the offensive split side tackle. If the tackle blocks inside, the weakside linebacker should step to the inside. The linebacker should never get hooked. As soon as the tackle sets up and shows pass, the linebacker should drop back to his assigned area. On a sweep, the linebacker should attack inside or outside of the defensive end. This depends upon the offensive tackle's block and the quickness of the sweep. If the defensive end uses a squeezing force charge, the linebacker is coached to attack the sweep outside of the defensive end (Diagram 6-20).

If the offensive tackle fires out directly into the weakside linebacker on a quick dive play, the defender should deliver a blow on the blocker, fight pressure, get rid of the blocker and attack the diving ball carrier (Diagram 6-21).

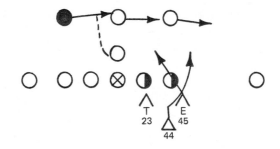

DIAGRAM 6-20

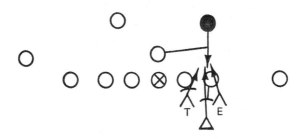

DIAGRAM 6-21

Outside Linebacker's Coaching Points ("44"):

1. Attack the run first and react to the pass second.
2. If a play action pass develops and you start to attack the ball, don't stop and play in between; continue to attack the man with the ball.
3. Turn the screen pass inside if the screen shows to the outside.
4. The revert linebacker is responsible for the linemen's alignment to his side.
5. If an offensive back shifts and lines up in a slot to the revert side, call for a knockdown technique and line up on the slot man according to his width from the tackle (Diagram 6-22).
6. If Triple Option is directed to the revert split side of the defense, the "44" linebacker is assigned to attack the dive man (Diagram 6-23).
7. If a sprint-out option shows, the revert linebacker is assigned to attack the quarterback as quickly as possible (Diagram 6-24).
8. If play goes away, check for the inside counter or draw play.

In the following chapter, the reader will learn how to coach the winning defensive stunts of the Fifty Bubble and Revert Defenses.

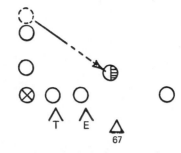

DIAGRAM 6-22
Knock-Down Call

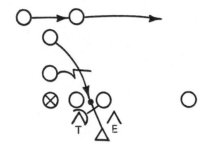

DIAGRAM 6-23

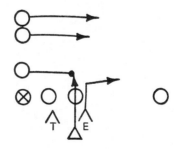

DIAGRAM 6-24

7

The Fifty Bubble and Revert Stunting Defenses

Defensive stunts are necessary to stop the opposition's bread and butter running plays or to take away their top passes by rushing the passer off his feet. Stunts and blitzes help break up the rhythm of an offensive drive and put pressure on the offensive blockers. The offensive blockers are now forced to block zones or areas rather than men, and this gives the defender an excellent chance to slip through to the ball carrier for a timely loss. We like to stunt or blitz especially to move an added defender to the offensive point of the attack.

When blitzing, the signal caller makes a "Lucky" call for a stunt to the left and a "Ringo" call for a stunt to the right. Without a stunt call or on a regular or normal call, the signal caller should make a false "Lucky" or "Ringo" signal call as the offense lines up. This false call will be meaningless to the defense, but will not alert the offense to a stunt, shift, or blitz whenever the signal caller calls his directions. We use the "Lucky" and "Ringo" calls for direction; this is not just a fancy term, but is used by the linebackers and defensive linemen to distinguish between the deep secondary's left and right calls. A mistake in direction by our secondary defenders may easily result in a quick offensive touchdown.

The linebackers should move around just prior to the snap of the ball to disguise the defense. The hard-nose calls signal the defenders to crowd up and closer to the ball. The hard-nose call is usually used on third and short-yardage and against a possible trap call by the opponent's offense.

At times when we face a team who likes to trap and pull guards, we allow the linebackers to fire in behind the pulling guards and run the ball carrier down from behind. This technique has caused many fumbles and has confused the opposition's blocking patterns on numerous occasions.

CRASH TECHNIQUE (Diagram 7-1)

Alignment: ''223.''

Stance: Two-point hitting position.

Key and Reaction: Key offensive movement and set a course for the outside shoulder of the tackle's original position. This stunt is used only if the ball goes toward the crashing linebacker.

Read: Read the outside-in block of the playside offensive tackle and end.

Responsibilities:

1. Blitz for the outside shoulder of the offensive tackle.
2. Fight the pressure of the block.
3. Dip the inside shoulder and keep the shoulders parallel to the line of scrimmage.
4. Come under control and be ready to react to the ball.
5. Pass: Drop-Back Pass—Hook area.
    Sprint To—Crash through predetermined course.
    Sprint Away—Relative hook, slide to opposite
        linebacker's zone assignment.

Coaching Point: ''Lucky'' linebacker should step to call side and continue through with his stunt. If flow is away, the linebacker should scallop toward the ball. The left defensive tackle must veer tight inside to

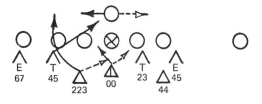

DIAGRAM 7-1
Crash Lucky (Revert)

a "23" position to the outside shoulder of the offensive guard's original position (Diagram 7-1).

DOUBLE CRASH (Diagram 7-2)

A Double Crash can only be called when we are lined up in a Fifty Bubble alignment. When this call is made, both of the tackles crash regardless of the flow of the quarterback, but the linebacker must key the quarterback's flow as they blitz only when action comes their way (Diagram 7-2).

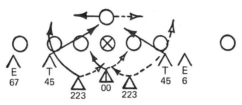

DIAGRAM 7-2
Double Crash (Bubble)

SQUEEZE TECHNIQUE (Diagram 7-3)

Alignment: "223."

Stance: Two-point hitting position.

Key and Reaction: Key offensive movement and set a course for the outside shoulder of the tight end's original position. This stunt is on only if the ball goes to the side of the stunt.

Read: Read the down block by the tight end.

Responsibilities:

1. Scrape for the outside shoulder of the tight end's original position.
2. Fight pressure of the tight end's block.
3. Dip inside shoulder and square shoulders to line of scrimmage once the "67" position is reached.
4. Come under control and be ready to react in any direction the ball moves.
5. Pass: Drop Back—Hook area.
     Sprint To—Scrape to "67" area and attack the passer.
     Sprint Away—Relative hook area and slide to the ball.

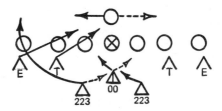

DIAGRAM 7-3
Squeeze Lucky (Bubble)

Coaching Point: This stunt is most advantageous against a sprint-out attack. It is a good call to the side of the anticipated sprint-out pass or sweep.

DOUBLE SQUEEZE (Diagram 7-4)

A Double Squeeze puts the pressure on the sprint-out pass in either sprint to or sprint away direction. Attacking the sprint-out pass from the backside is one of the finest rushes that can be executed against the sprint-out attack.

Coaching Point: In the Double Squeeze call, the middle linebacker must decide which is the most dangerous side and keep the outside forearm free to that side. The Double Squeeze call is an excellent call against the sweeping or sprint-out offensive attack.

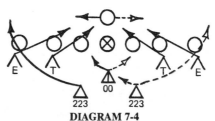

DIAGRAM 7-4
Double Squeeze (Bubble)

BLAST STUNT LUCKY (Diagram 7-5)

The Blast Stunt Lucky is used from the regular Bubble alignment. When the Blast technique is called, the tackle and the end to the side of the blast loop to the outside and the two linebackers blitz into the gap to the call side. For example: "Blast Lucky" calls for the left linebacker to blitz into the "3" gap to the left side, while the backside linebacker blitzes into the "1" gap to the left side. The middle linebacker is assigned to stunt into the "1" gap away from the call side. The right tackle and the right defensive end play their regular Bubble assignments and techniques (Diagram 7-5).

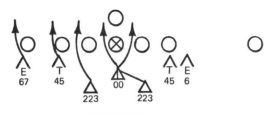

DIAGRAM 7-5
Blast Lucky (Bubble)

TWIN BLAST RINGO (Diagram 7-6)

A Twin Blast Ringo Stunt may also be called when the two normal inside linebackers are assigned to a twin alignment. In this twin alignment, the right linebacker lines up in his normal "223" alignment, and the left linebacker moves over to the right side and lines up in an "11" alignment. From these two linebacker alignments, both the linebackers blitz straight ahead into their respective gaps. The middle linebacker loops into the left "1" gap, and both the defensive right tackle and end loop to their outside positions. The defensive left tackle and left end play their regular techniques.

The reason the Twin Blast is used is to give the offensive attack another defensive alignment look. It also affords the defensive backside

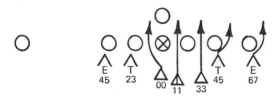

DIAGRAM 7-6
Twin Blast Ringo (Twin Bubble)

linebacker a chance to fire into the "1" gap more quickly from his "11" alignment than from his normal backside "223" alignment. If the ball goes away from the twin alignment call or a drop-back pass develops, the blitzing linebackers and stunting defenders still go through their blitz call and then pursue the ball. Once the ball has been located, the defenders are coached to take their proper pursuit course and cut off the ball (Diagram 7-6).

Coaching Point: The signal caller's call is usually directed toward the tight end's side. The middle linebacker and inside linebackers should continually move around so that they can disguise their intentions and their alignments.

TWIN REGULAR RINGO (Diagram 7-7)

The Twin Regular call is used as a change-up alignment from the Twin Blast Blitz. Thus, the Twin Regular linebackers line up in their same alignments as the Twin Blast alignment, but they do not blitz. On the snap of the ball, the linebackers shuffle back to their normal "223" alignments and are responsible for their normal "223" techniques. The middle linebacker, who is offset in the Lucky "1" gap, steps back into the center with a solid forearm and then plays a normal "0" technique and fights the pressure of the center's block and locates the ball. Both of the defensive tackles and defensive ends play their regular defensive alignments and techniques (Diagram 7-7).

DIAGRAM 7-7
Twin Regular Ringo (Twin Bubble)

DEFENSIVE LINEBACKER TECHNIQUES—REGULAR "223" TECHNIQUE

Alignment: "223"—split the outside leg of the offensive guard.

Stance: Two-point-hitting or football position.

Key and Reaction:

1. Key the offensive guard through to the ball.
2. Never get hooked in by the offensive guard.

Read: Read the blocking of the guard-center and tackle triangular pattern.

Responsibilities:

1. Deliver a blow on the guard.
2. Fight pressure.
3. Get rid of the blocker.
4. If Play Away: Scallop and get into pursuit course.
5. Pass: Drop Back—Hook area.
      Sprint To—Relative hook area.
      Sprint Away—Relative hook area, slide to opposite linebacker's zone assignment.

"223" Linebacker's Pass Defense:

Drop Back Passes: The linebacker should sprint back to his hook zone ten yards in front of the offensive tight end's original position and check for the hook pass. If no one shows in the hook area, the "223" linebacker is coached to shuffle to the curl zone and look for a potential receiver in that area. The linebacker should focus his eyes on the passer, while retreating into his area by sprinting back on a 45 degree angle, watching the passer over his inside shoulder (Diagram 7-8).

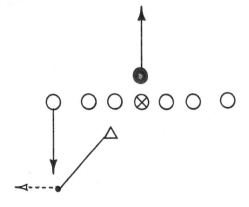

DIAGRAM 7-8

If a sprint-out pass is run in the direction of the "223" linebacker, he is coached to sprint back to his hook assignment and continue moving to keep head up on the moving quarterback. If a receiver should cross the linebacker's face, he is taught to knock the receiver down as long as the pass has not been thrown. If another pass defender's flat assignment has been predetermined, the "223" linebacker now has the option of defending against the pass or attacking the passer (Diagram 7-9).

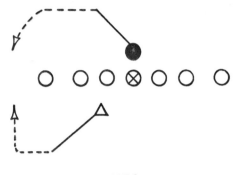

DIAGRAM 7-9

If a sprint-out or bootleg pass action is run away from the "223" linebacker, the linebacker is coached to retreat to the hook zone. As soon as the potential passer or ball carrier crosses the imaginary end box, the backside linebacker is coached to leave his assigned hook area and begin to sprint toward the ball (Diagram 7-10). The linebacker should look for any potential crossing or dragging receivers and knock them down if they cross his face.

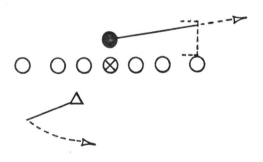

DIAGRAM 7-10

The linebackers are coached to play the run first and the pass second. Therefore, on any play action pass, the linebacker must first defend against the run. If the linebacker is fooled by one of the faking backs and finds himself on the line of scrimmage as a pass develops, he should continue through with his attacking route and rush the passer. We never want any of our defenders trying to play an "in between position." The "in between position" is that of hanging on the line of scrimmage and not rushing the passer or defending against the receiver. Our coaching staff tells the defenders we want a firm defensive commitment. When in doubt, we tell our linebackers to rush the passer.

Coaching Note: The linebackers must be taught that their zones change as the passer sprints to or away from their respective positions. All linebackers must be taught to move with the passer in the direction of their new extended zone assignment.

DEFENSIVE TACKLE—REGULAR "45" TECHNIQUE

Alignment: "45" alignment, lining up splitting the outside foot of the offensive tackle with the midline of the defender's body. Depth off the ball depends upon defense called, down, distance, score, etc.

Stance: Four-point stance.

Key and Reaction: Key the hand of the offensive tackle. Move on movement. Explode a forearm under the offensive tackle's shoulder pads. Try to keep him off the linebacker. Keep the shoulders square to the line of scrimmage. Get rid of the blocker as soon as possible.

Read: Read the block of the tackle; then read the block of the tight end or near back on the move. As the offensive tackle steps down, the defender should close and check for the trap. If the tackle blocks out, fight pressure and attack the blocker.

Responsibilities:
1. Explode into the tackle with the inside forearm.
2. Step with the inside foot.
3. Don't give up ground to a double team block.
4. Keep the outside arm free.
5. Maintain a relative rush against the pass.
6. Attack: (a) Play To—Fight pressure of the block and attack the play from the inside-out angle.

(b) Play Away—Pursue the ball going through the blocker's head.

(c) Drop-Back Pass—Attack passer, use a relative rush.

A more extensive explanation of the defensive tackle's "45" keys, reactions, reads, and responsibilities may be found in "Coaching Forty Over and Under Defense," in *Football's Fabulous Forty Defense,* by Jack Olcott (Parker Publishing Company, Inc., West Nyack, New York, 1974).

DEFENSIVE END—REGULAR "67" TECHNIQUE

Alignment: "67" alignment, lining up splitting the outside foot of the offensive end with the midline of the defender's body. Depth off the line of scrimmage depends upon the defense called, down, distance, score, etc.

Stance: Two-point stance. The inside foot should be up and the defender should be in a balanced football hitting position.

Key and Reaction: Key the helmet of the offensive end. Step with the inside foot and deliver a blow with the same arm. Keep the shoulders square to the line of scrimmage. Play the off-tackle hole. Get heel depth, locate the ball, and attack the ball carrier.

Read: Read the offensive end's and the tackle's block. Check the blocking pattern of an inside-out block by a pulling lineman.

Responsibilities:

1. Explode into the end with an inside forearm.
2. Step with the inside foot.
3. Close down to the inside, if the end steps down.
4. Force-contain the ball carrier.
5. Maintain inside pressure.
6. Keep the shoulders square to the line of scrimmage.
7. Attack the ball carrier; don't wait for him to attack.
8. Stop the off-tackle play from an outside-in angle.

A more extensive explanation of the defensive end's "67" keys, reactions, reads, and responsibilities may be found in "Coaching Forty Over and Under Defenses," in *Football's Fabulous Forty Defense* by

Jack Olcott, (Parker Publishing Company, Inc., West Nyack, New York, 1974).

REVERT STUNTS

Whenever the defense jumps from the Bubble Defense to the Revert Defense (Diagram 7-11), we use two weakside stunts that are the same as our other weakside stunts, only now, the stunts are employed from a different alignment. The Revert "1" Blitz is similar is similar to the Fifty-one off the Fifty Knockdown look (Diagram 7-12). The difference

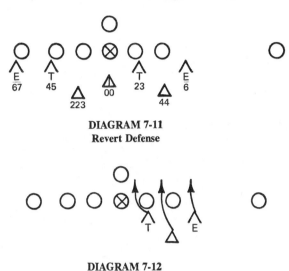

DIAGRAM 7-11
Revert Defense

DIAGRAM 7-12
Revert 1

between the Fifty-one blitzes and the Revert "1" Blitz is that the linebacker blitzes from his "44" alignment instead of from an outside "6" alignment. Another stunt to the short side is the Squeeze Ringo blitz which features the defensive tackle pinching to the shoulder of the center and the defensive end angling in to the outside shoulder of the offensive weak guard. The linebacker then scrapes off to the original position of the offensive tackle's outside shoulder. As soon as the weakside linebacker reaches the "45" area, he is taught to square off his shoulders to the line of scrimmage and be ready to move in any direction to attack the ball carrier (Diagram 7-13).

The tight side stunts include the Crash call, which is used similarly to the Bubble Crash with the defensive strong side tackle crashing to the outside shoulder of the strong side offensive guard, while the "223" linebacker scrapes off to the defensive tackle's original alignment "67" (Diagram 7-14). The Blast Blitz is also used, but, because of the alignment of the linebackers in the Revert Defense, we use a Half Blast Blitz. The "half" means that only one linebacker blitzes to the opposite side of the step-around technique by the middle linebacker (Diagram 7-15).

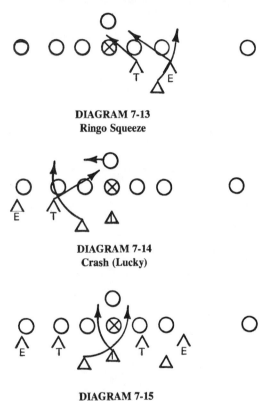

DIAGRAM 7-13
Ringo Squeeze

DIAGRAM 7-14
Crash (Lucky)

DIAGRAM 7-15
Revert—Half Blast (Ringo)

Another stunt off the Revert Defense is the Barrel Lucky Blitz, which features both the strong side linebacker and the middle linebacker blitzing the gaps to their left.

All the other defenders play their regular defensive technique (Diagram 7-16). This is a fine stunt to combine the Revert "1" or Squeeze Stunt to the split side of the offensive formation.

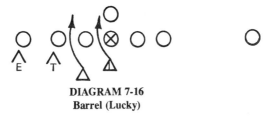

DIAGRAM 7-16
Barrel (Lucky)

A new stunt that is used off the Revert look (may also be used off the Bubble Defense) is the Fold Lucky stunt. This stunt blitzes the left linebacker directly over the right shoulder of the offensive center on the snap of the ball. The middle linebacker is coached to take a set or delayed step and then cut off the tail of the blitzing left linebacker into the "23" area. Once the middle linebacker reaches the "3" gap, he checks for the ball. If the ball is going in the same direction as his stunt, he continues on and attempts to cut off the ball carrier (Diagram 7-17). If the play goes away when the middle linebacker reaches the "3" gap, the linebacker is coached to come under control and take a flat course or adjust his angle so that he will be able to head off the ball carrier.

Many of these stunts may be combined. For example, the signal caller may call "Crash Lucky and Squeeze Ringo" (Diagram 7-18).

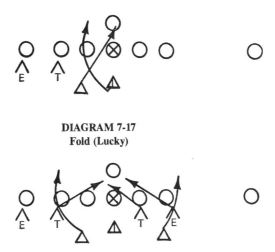

DIAGRAM 7-17
Fold (Lucky)

DIAGRAM 7-18
Crash (Lucky)—Squeeze (Ringo)

8

How to Coach the Fifty-three Pro Defense

This eight-man front (Pro Fifty-three Defense) is normally a containing defense, but it can also be used as a strong stunting or blitzing defense. We still like to use the Fifty-three Pro versus the opposition's favorite third down passing plays. With a quick, aggressive and solid middle linebacker, this defense often confuses many of the more modern offensive attacks with the middle linebacker unblocked. These new blocking rules often make the five-three defense an exception to their regular line blocking rules. Therefore, the Fifty-three Pro Defense, if used as a surprise, often confuses the more conservative offensive attacks.

This defense can be easily adjusted to any of the modern offensive formations.

The Fifty-three Pro Defense is an even defense featuring three linebackers, which is the reason we call it the Fifty-three defense. In it, we move the middle guard from a normal "0" alignment in our regular Fifty Defense to a "2" alignment. The middle guard always lines up to his left side or to the offensive strong side, if the offense declares a particular strong side formation (Diagram 8-1). If the offensive formation employs a split end, we may move the outside linebacker, in a "667" position (Diagram 8-1), to a regular adjusted linebacker position, as illustrated in Diagram 8-2.

The Fifty-three Pro Defense features a three-deep secondary. This three-deep pass defense can play a locked-in defense (straight three-deep—no revolving). The three-deep defense can also revolve, leveling

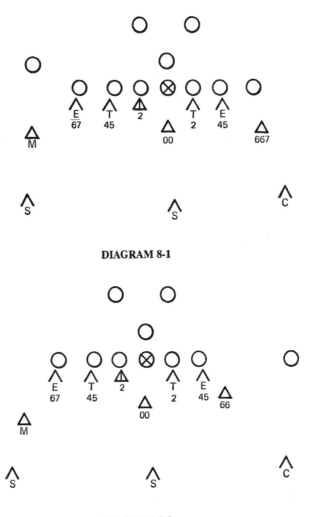

DIAGRAM 8-1

DIAGRAM 8-2

off one of the deep defenders into the flat with the other two deep defenders playing the deep areas alone.

The Responsibility Chart pertaining to the Fifty-three Pro Defense affords the reader an outline of the alignment, keys by progression, and responsibilities. The responsibility pictured in Diagram 8-3 shows each of the seven-man defensive front their points or area of responsibility in diagram form. (See Diagrams 8-3a, 8-3b and 8-3c.)

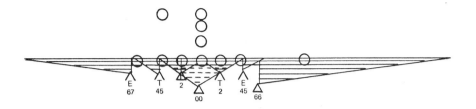

POSITION	ALIGNMENT	KEYS BY PROGRESSION	RESPONSIBILITY
STRONG END	67	(1) End	Original position of end to sidelines
OUTSIDE LINEBACKER	66	(2) Near Back	
		(3) Fullback	
STRONG TACKLE	45	(1) Tackle	Nose of tackle to nose of end
		(2) End	
WEAK ENDS		(3) Near Back	
GUARD	2	(1) Guard	Nose of guard to nose of center
WEAK TACKLE		(2) Center	
		(3) Fullback	
MIDDLE LINEBACKER	00	(1) Quarterback	Nose of center to nose of tackle to each side
		(2) Fullback	
		(3) Halfback	

DIAGRAM 8-3a

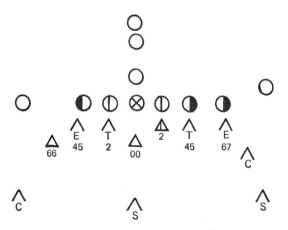

DIAGRAM 8-3b

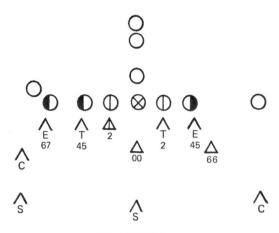

DIAGRAM 8-3c

OUTSIDE LINEBACKER "667" AND END "67" TO THE TIGHT END'S SIDE "67" (Diagram 8-1)

The outside linebacker and end must line up in the regular "67" and "667" positions, splitting the tight end's outside foot with the midline between their feet. Their key is the near back through the tight end. These (the "67" and "667" defenders) are responsible for closing down on the power off-tackle plays and must "chug" the end if he tries to release to the defender's inside. The "67" and "667" defenders must be able to defeat the tight end's reach or cut-off block. Two methods we use are: (1) The defensive linebacker and end should use a two-hand shiver (with the inside arm on the tight end's head and the outside arm on the tight end's outside shoulder), locking the elbows to keep the blocker away from the defender's wheels (legs). (2) The defender should use the inside arm thrust up and through the blocker's neck and face mask, while stepping with the inside leg to his outside area. Against the off-tackle play, the defender must close down as soon as the tight end steps to the inside. If the tight end tries to release to the inside, the defensive linebacker and end must jam the potential receiver and then continue with the all-out rush on the passer or cover the defense pass assignment, depending upon the secondary pass coverage call.

END AND TACKLE TO THE TIGHT END'S SIDE "45" (Diagram 8-1)

The defensive end and tackle should line up in their four-point stances, splitting the outside leg of the strong side offensive tackle in their regular "45" alignment. The defensive tackle and end must protect their outside legs by using a forearm blow with the inside arms, keeping their outside arms free to get rid of the head-on block or to ward off the potential down-blocking tight end.

If the strong offensive tackle attempts to reach block the "45" defender, he must shuffle to the outside and make a quick defensive read. The defensive read off the reach block is usually a sweep, quick pitch, or sprint-out pass to the strong side. The defender must make his quick read because he must be ready to adjust his pursuit course depending upon the path of the ball carrier. If pass shows, he must use his contain-rush technique.

If the offensive tackle blocks to the inside (toward the offensive center), the "45" defender must look for the tight end's down block, trap by the guard, or turn-out block by one of the offensive backs.

DEFENSIVE TACKLE AND MIDDLE GUARD TECHNIQUES "2" (Diagram 8-1)

The defensive tackle and middle guard play to both the tight and split end's side is similar. The "2" defender must be ready to handle the one-on-one block by the offensive guard, the double team block, reach block, fold block, cross block, and the quick trap block.

If the defensive tackle is blocked head on by the offensive guard, he must move on movement, deliver a blow, fight pressure of the head-on block; then he must read the ball carrier and get into the correct pursuit pattern.

When the offense attempts to double team the defensive tackle or middle guard, they must anchor the defense by holding their ground. The best technique to use is to fight the power block by staying low on all fours, fight the blocker's pressure, and then attempt to split the blockers.

If the offensive blocker attempts to reach block the "2" defender, he should use his hands to keep the blocker away from his feet. We teach the defender to force the blocker's helmet into the ground, using a straight-arm shiver. Then he must fight through the blocker's head, using his inside arm lift to blast up and through the potential reach blocker.

The "2" defender is taught to fight the tackle's down block whenever the offensive line attempts to use the fold block against our Fifty-three Defense. The "45" defender must keep his shoulders parallel to the goal line as he fights the outside blocker's drive block. This is the same technique we use versus the offensive cross block.

If the offense attacks the "2" defender on a quick short trap play, the defender must close toward the center and meet the blocker with his inside forearm. The defender's shoulders should be parallel to the line of scrimmage, and he should read the ball carrier's path as he meets the trapping guard.

DEFENSIVE END TO SPLIT END'S SIDE "45" (Diagram 8-4)

The defensive end lines up splitting the tackle's outside foot ("45" alignment). He should use a two-point stance with the outside foot back, reading through the short side tackle to the near back. If the linebacker to the short side lines up inside the "45" defender, the "45" defender must be the contain man. If the linebacker lines up outside the "45" defender to the short side (split end's side), the linebacker has the contain assignment. The "45" defender must never be hooked and must be ready to close off the inside dive play if the offensive tackle closes down to the inside. The defensive end must keep his shoulders parallel to the line of scrimmage and keep the blocking offensive tackle away from his legs with his forearm or his two-arm shiver. As soon as he closes down, following the offensive tackle's down block, the defensive end must look for the near back's quick dive play.

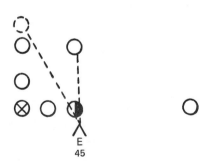

DIAGRAM 8-4

If the split side tackle attempts to reach block the "45" defender, he must use his two-arm shiver and shuffle to the outside, looking for the ball carrier. If the offensive tackle shoots his head across the body of the defensive end, the "45" defender should use his inside forearm lift up and through the potential blocker's neck. This forces the defender to go directly through the blocker's head, moving upfield with his shoulders parallel to the line of scrimmage.

If the split side offensive tackle attempts to turn out the defensive end, the "45" defender must fight straight through the blocker's pressure and attack the ball carrier.

REVERT LINEBACKER "44" (Diagram 8-5)

The split side linebacker may line up in a "44" alignment (Diagram 8-5). The split side linebacker reads the near side running back. In our man-to-man pass coverage call, he takes this offensive running back man to man which allows our weakside safetyman to be free to roam the secondary. The linebackers must be ready to attack the near back on a quick dive and also to scrape off and be ready to help contain the outside offensive plays.

If the near side running back takes off on his quick pitch course, the "44" linebacker is in perfect position to stop the play as he is assigned to key the near side running back. When the opposition runs a power or tear sweep to the split side, the linebacker is taught to keep his nose directly on the middle of the ball carrier and be ready to attack the ball carrier as soon as he makes his cut, with his shoulders parallel to the line of scrimmage.

If a straight drop-back pass develops and the secondary signal caller has made a zone call, the "44" linebacker must drop back on an outside 45 degree angle to take away the split end's curl pattern. If the split end catches a quick look-in pass, the linebacker must hit him so hard that the split end will not want to catch another quick pass. The split side linebacker's basic assignment is to take away the opponent's split side inside running attack. Therefore, he must defend against the inside plays first and pursue the outside plays second.

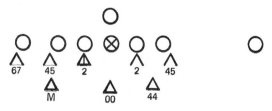

DIAGRAM 8-5

MIDDLE LINEBACKER "00" (Diagram 8-1)

The middle linebacker "00" lines up in a two-point breakdown football position approximately two yards off the line of scrimmage. He is assigned to key the head of the center and to read the offensive triangle (quarterback and both running backs). Once the ball has been put into play, he must attack plays from offensive tackle to tackle with his shoulders parallel to the goal line. The middle linebacker must be continually drilled to scallop (shuffle) along the line of scrimmage, checking each hole, so that he can step up and tackle the ball carrier with his shoulders squared to the line of scrimmage.

If the ball carrier goes wide, the middle linebacker is taught never to overrun the ball carrier. In order to defend against the cut-back maneuver by the ball carrier, we teach the middle linebacker always to stay a step behind the ball carrier. The outside contain man is assigned to force the ball carrier back into the pursuing middle linebacker so that he may meet the ball carrier head on with his shoulders parallel to the line of scrimmage.

If the quarterback drops straight back in his pocket, the middle linebacker is assigned to drop back favoring the hook zone to the tight end's side, if he is in a zone defensive pass call. When a sprint-out pass is called, he is taught to drop back at a 45 degree angle in the direction of the sprint-out pass. He must stay a step behind the quarterback in order to stop the sprint-out draw to the running back.

FIFTY-THREE STRONG PRO ADJUSTMENT

The Fifty-three Strong Pro Defense is a simple adjustment against a team that runs primarily to the strong side of their offensive formation. Utilizing a swing monster or rover back, we simply stack this defender directly behind the strong side defensive end. Many of our opponents have referred to this defense as a stacked defense because we often drop the weakside linebacker off the line, to a revert position, to the split end's side (Diagram 8-5), but against two tight ends, it remains a Fifty-three Pro Defense with a monster stack (Diagram 8-5a.)

This defense can be easily adjusted to any offensive formation, and is flexible enough to stop the most diversified offensive attack. The three-deep secondary makes this a balanced defense with the ability to stunt in the secondary as well as along the line of scrimmage. Actually

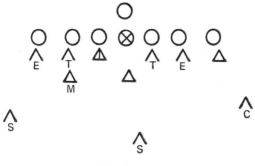

DIAGRAM 8-5a

this Fifty-three Strong Pro Defense has the same basic concepts as the Fifty Oklahoma Monster Defense.

The Strong Pro is an excellent defense against the sweeping offenses as well as the sprint-out teams. Against the sprint-out attack, it puts four quick rushers to the strong side of the offensive attack and affords the secondary to level the playside corner or halfback into the flat area. This is the most outstanding method of attacking a sprint-out team with a four-man rush, a defender in the flat, and a deep secondary defender covering the deep outside one-third zone (Diagram 8-6).

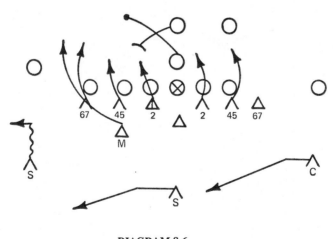

DIAGRAM 8-6

This defense is also strong against the successful power off-tackle teams. With the rover (monster) to the strong side of the opponent's formation, a blitz by the rover along with some gap charges by the defensive linemen help to cut off the power tackle play (Diagram 8-7).

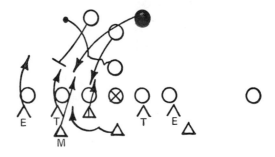

DIAGRAM 8-7

As soon as a play goes away from the monster back, the middle linebacker can fly out of his position toward the weakside with the defensive monster checking the middle counter area, directly over the center, as the linebacker scallops toward the weakside flow (Diagram 8-8).

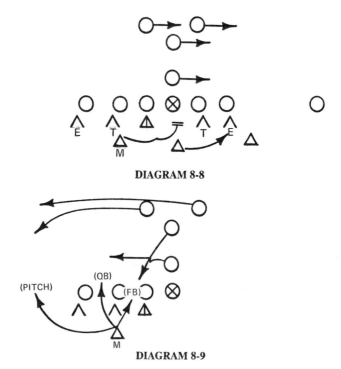

DIAGRAM 8-8

DIAGRAM 8-9

The monster alignment is also strong whenever the opponent tries to run a triple option play to the strong side. Using the Fifty-three Strong Pro alignment enables the rover back to attack the fullback, quarterback, or pitchman. The stacked position of the monster man makes him a difficult read for the triple optioning quarterback (Diagram 8-9).

THE FIFTY-THREE PRO VERSUS THE TRIPLE OPTION

One method of playing the triple option is by using the "feathering technique" while playing the Fifty-three Pro Defense. This technique is often used to the short or split end's side of the defense while using the "knocked down" adjustment (Diagram 8-10).

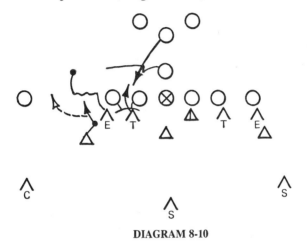

DIAGRAM 8-10

The defensive end plays the quarterback "lightly," thus the term "feathering" is used to describe the defensive end playing the quarterback an arm's distance away. The defensive end is taught to retreat away from the quarterback after the ball handler has faked to the fullback. The defensive end continues to retreat backward along the line of scrimmage as long as he can see both shoulders of the quarterback. The defender stays an arm's length away from the quarterback until he sees only one shoulder, then he attacks the quarterback with a smashing tackle. The coaching point behind attacking the quarterback as soon as the defensive man sees only one shoulder means the quarterback has turned his body parallel to the line of scrimmage and has decided to keep the ball (Diagram 8-11).

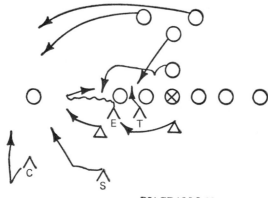

DIAGRAM 8-11

Using the feathering technique means the defensive tackle and the middle linebacker are responsible to stop the fullback dive; therefore, the middle linebacker must be coached to keep his head directly on the ball. If he overruns the play, the fullback will break the play for a long gainer.

The outside linebacker is responsible for containing the wide triple option pitch to the backside halfback. The defensive secondary, whether in a zone or man-to-man call, are responsible for aiding in containing the triple option pitch, stopping the quarterback keeper, or attacking the fullback dive.

This is another coaching point change-up in defending the triple option to the short or split end's side. This change-up helps to confuse the optioning quarterback by immediately attacking the quarterback at one moment, and then using the feathering technique the next time the offense runs the triple option. The reason our defensive staff likes the feathering technique is that the defense plays the waiting game on the line of scrimmage and makes the quarterback make up his mind on a delayed stringing-out basis. The longer it takes the quarterback to make up his mind, the stronger opportunity the defense has to stop the triple option attack with pursuit. After interviewing several outstanding triple optioning quarterbacks and offensive backfield coaches, we have found these men feel that this style of defensive play is the most consistent defense against the triple option attack. This type of defensive strategy enables the defense to take away the best offensive back!

Another method of changing up the defensive attack against the triple option is the safetyman blitz. The safetyman is coached to attack the quarterback, since the defensive end in his "45" technique has the assignment of tackling the fullback from his outside-in angle. The outside linebacker in his "6" alignment is responsible for containing the pitchman with the outside cornerman's assignment as secondary containment. The middle linebacker "00" has three check points: first, he must check the fullback for the ball; second, he checks the quarterback for a possible keeper; third, he must be in position to attack the pitchman if the ball carrier attempts to cut inside the frontside offensive back's block (Diagram 8-12).

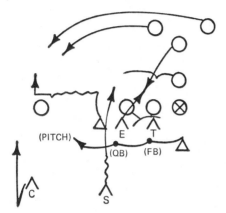

DIAGRAM 8-12

The main reason we like to use the safety blitz on the quarterback is that his first key is the "45" defender. Once the "45" defender attacks the fullback, the quarterback keeps the ball and checks the outside linebacker "6." As soon as he sees the end man "6" on the line of scrimmage containing, the quarterback is taught to keep the ball. When this happens, the safetyman comes up and hits the quarterback from the blind side. This blitzing maneuver often causes a fumble by the surprised quarterback (Diagram 8-12).

COORDINATING THE FIFTY-ONE PRO LINEBACKERS' DEFENSIVE PASS RESPONSIBILITIES

If an opponent continually attempts to flood or throw short to the strong or tight end's side, we use a special call to coordinate our front defenders' zone coverage areas. A predetermined "King" call tells our linebackers we will use an overbalanced, underneath, coverage call to the strong side of the formation. This call actually means that our strong end to the strong or tight end's side and our middle linebacker will go from their predetermined underneath zone call to a man-to-man call as soon as the front side number three man breaks the "67" plane or runs into a pattern outside of the tight end's original positon (Diagram 8-13). This

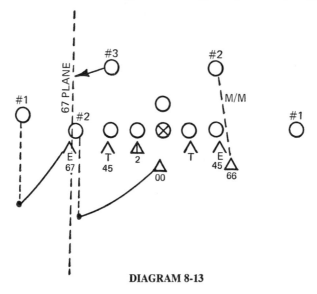

DIAGRAM 8-13

means the defensive strong end is responsible to cover the number three man as soon as he crosses the "67" plane (Diagram 8-14). The number three man is covered by the middle linebacker if he does not cross the "67" plane (Diagram 8-15).

The vocal coordination begins between the secondary as soon as the potential pass receivers make their cuts. In Diagram 8-14 the defensive cornerman would yell, "Swing, swing," to help the strong end, while the inside strong safetyman would holler, "Hook, hook," to help the middle linebacker in picking up the hooking tight end. All three of these diagrams (8-13, 8-14, and 8-15) are "King Lucky" calls. (*Coaching note:* Secondary calls are very important for the linebackers and strong end because these defenders drop back with their eyes on the quarterback.)

If the opponent switches his pass patterns and attempts to flood the receivers to his weak or split end side, our middle linebacker now makes a

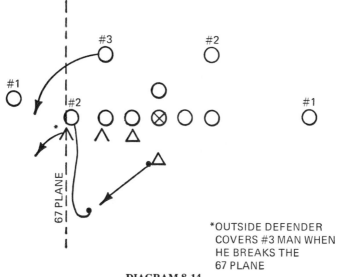

*OUTSIDE DEFENDER
COVERS #3 MAN WHEN
HE BREAKS THE
67 PLANE

DIAGRAM 8-14
King Left Call (Lucky)

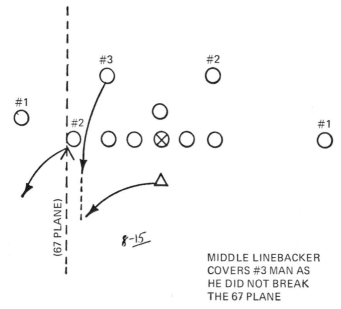

MIDDLE LINEBACKER
COVERS #3 MAN AS
HE DID NOT BREAK
THE 67 PLANE

DIAGRAM 8-15
King Left Call (Lucky)

"Queen" call. The "Queen" call directs our overbalanced linebacker defensive flow to the opponent's weak or split end side (Diagram 8-16).

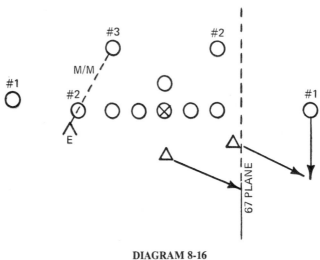

DIAGRAM 8-16
Queen Right (All Ringo)

All of the defensive rules in "Queen Ringo" are the same as the linebackers' rules in "King Lucky" illustrated in Diagrams 8-13, 8-14, and 8-15. Therefore, the "King" call directs our linebackers to flow to the opponent's strong or tight end side, and the "Queen" call sends the flow of the defensive end and linebackers to the weak or split end side of the offensive formation.

On both the above calls, the middle linebacker is still responsible for all middle draws. He must key the offensive center because the pivot man is normally assigned to block the middle linebacker on most middle draws. A coaching point we use to read draw for the middle linebacker is to key the offensive center's first two steps. On a normal drop-back pocket pass, the center will use a set step and then come up high to set up in his normal pocket pass protection stance. If the center is assigned to block the middle linebacker, he will set step on his first step and then fire low directly at the middle linebacker, or he may disregard the set step and fire out immediately at the middle linebacker. The middle linebacker is coached to read the center's low fire-out technique, ward off the pivot man's block, and then make the tackle on the draw ball carrier.

STRONG SIDE DEFENSIVE END'S "67" PASS DROP AREA

As soon as pass shows, the defensive end is taught to drop back into his assigned zone if a defensive zone call has been assigned to the linebacker corps. Regardless of whether a roll-out, sprint-out, or a scramble pattern develops toward the strong end position, Diagram 8-17 illus-

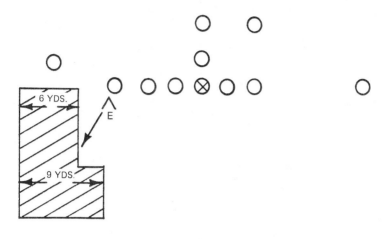

DIAGRAM 8-17

trates an area which is taboo for the strong end to be in until the pass is in the air. Therefore, whenever the strong defensive end is near to the sidelines, he is directed to stay six yards away from the sideline, fifteen yards deep to the goal line prior to the passer throwing the ball (Diagram 8-17).

The exception to this rule is whenever the outside linebacker is called into a double coverage alignment, in which case the linebacker uses either his jolt and drop or bump and run technique. (See linebacker's double cover techniques, Diagram 8-23.)

PLAY AWAY FROM THE STRONG END FIFTY-THREE PRO DEFENDER

As soon as play goes away from the defensive end, he is coached to flow two yards behind the defensive end's original position. Once he reaches this point, referred to by our defensive staff as the Counter Point, he is coached to check for counters, reverses, and bootleg plays coming back against the flow of the offense (Diagram 8-18).

The defensive end is coached to chase the ball just a yard shallower than the ball. The linebacker, after reaching his counter point, is taught to continue through his pursuit pattern to cut off the ball carrier as long as flow continues away from the counter point (Diagram 8-18).

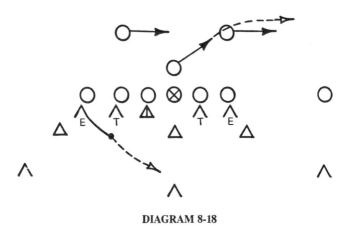

DIAGRAM 8-18

SHORT SIDE (SPLIT SIDE) LINEBACKER DEFENDING THE PASS

The professional method used to defend against the pass by the short side or weakside linebacker is to shuffle backward as soon as the quarter-back shows pass, watching the receiver rather than the passer. This means the short side or split side linebacker turns his head and focuses on the route of the near halfbacks. If the halfback flares and the split end crosses in front of the linebacker's face, the linebacker is coached to knock the split end down, or at least get a piece of him.

If the split end attempts to run a curl pattern, the pro-type linebacker is coached to sprint back, keeping his eyes on the split end, and get in front of the curling potential receiver and then look for the ball (Diagram 8-19). If the split end runs a sideline pass pattern, the outside split side or short side linebacker is coached to sprint to a point between the potential pass receiver and the split end, so that his defensive position will force the passer to arch the football over the linebacker's head. This will make the pass more susceptible to an interception by one of the deeper defensive backs (Diagram 8-20).

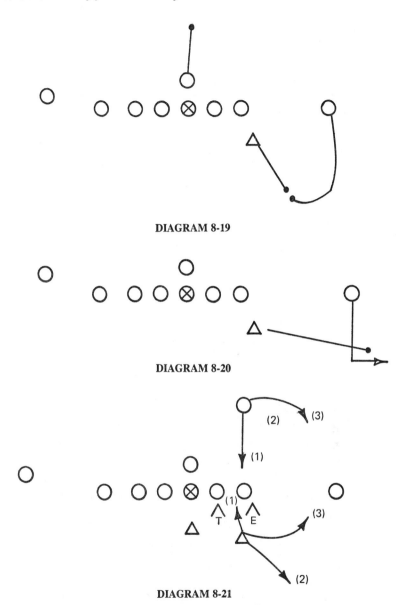

DIAGRAM 8-19

DIAGRAM 8-20

DIAGRAM 8-21

There are times when the pro-type outside linebacker is assigned to defend against the near or weakside running back, using an assigned man-to-man pass defensive "44" technique. This is usually used with the weakside safetyman in a free safetyman's role (Diagram 8-21). If the near side back sets up to block the outside linebacker, the defender should take a set step to check for the halfback draw and then sprint back into the outside flat zone. Whenever the defensive quarterback calls for the defense to use an invert coverage to the side of the split end, the linebacker is coached to automatically rush the passer, because we do not want two pass defenders in the same flat zone (Diagram 8-22).

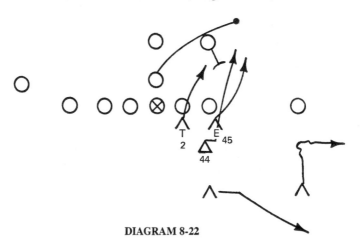

DIAGRAM 8-22

WEAKSIDE LINEBACKER'S ADJUSTED POSITIONS

Double Cover Call (Diagram 8-23): If a double cover call has been made, the defender is coached to stay two yards off the wide receiver and chug him to keep him off his intended pass course. Usually the doubling defender will use a chug to force the potential receiver to the inside. Using this technique, he lines up on the outside shoulder of the wide

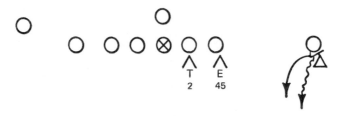

DIAGRAM 8-23

receiver. The defender is taught to use the bump and run technique usually up to a ten-yard depth. If no receiver enters his zone, the defender continues to shuffle backward as long as the passer stays in his pocket.

Hold-up Call "65" (Diagram 8-24): The linebacker uses this call against the tight end when a passing down is expected. The defender lines up in a "65" position, using a parallel stance with his toes parallel to the defensive end's toes. The defender is taught to hit aggressively and hold up the tight end. Once the tight end releases, the linebacker is coached to shadow him back to the hook area. The defensive end lines up in a "67" position and hits the tight end also. Both the defenders force the tight end to break through the middle of the two receivers. Then the defensive end is assigned to rush the passer.

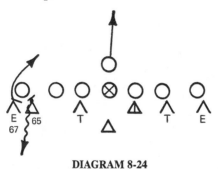

DIAGRAM 8-24

Walk-Away (Diagram 8-25): At times the weakside linebacker may be called upon to line up in a walk-away position. This assignment depends upon the defensive game plan. The walk-away assignment will be assigned each game.

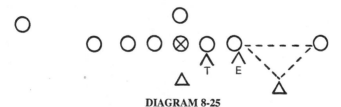

DIAGRAM 8-25

Revert Position "44": When playing the revert position, the linebacker should key the end. He should support the off-tackle play from an outside-in angle, and is responsible to support the sweep. If the near back attempts to run a divide pattern, breaking the seam between the deep zones, the reverted linebacker "44" should drop to the hook area and then slide to the curl area if no one shows in his assigned hook area (Diagram 8-26). As the linebacker drops back into his hook area, he should key the near back and cover him man to man into the flat if a Level or Roll call has not been made to his side (Diagram 8-27). If a Level call has been made, the linebacker should continue to cover the curl zone (Diagram 8-28).

The Fifty-three Defense takes on a "stacked look" in the next chapter.

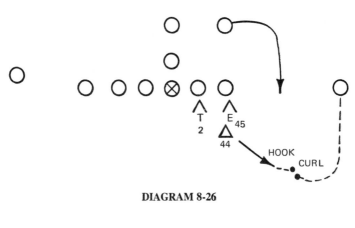

DIAGRAM 8-26

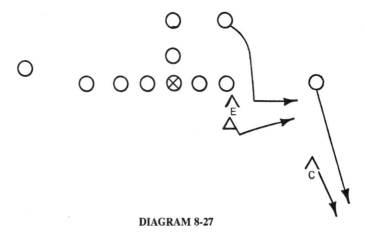

DIAGRAM 8-27

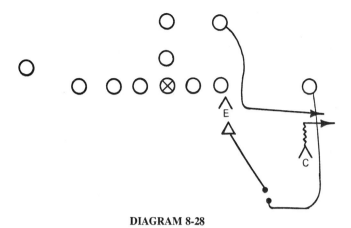

DIAGRAM 8-28

9

Teaching the Fifty-three Stack Defense

The Fifty-three Stack Defense is an excellent defense against both the pass and the strong off-tackle and inside running defense. Against the pass, the straight three-deep, locked-in secondary defense minimizes the pass defenders' chances of missing any rolling or inverting techniques because of the consistency of the secondary's assignments. It is also a solid blitzing defense with three linebackers ready to attack the passer. Against the inside offensive attack, the three linebackers stacked behind their down linemen give this defense a six-to-five defensive ratio over the offensive line from tackle to tackle. The various blitzes and stunts off the Fifty-three Stacked Defense enable our defenders to throw the offense for losses and confuse their offensive blocking assignments.

A quick glance at the Fifty-three Stacked Defense Responsibility Chart enables the reader to gain a concise comprehensive view of this defense's alignment, keys, and defensive responsibilities (Diagram 9-1).

The Fifty-three Stack Defense utilizes a five-man line (one inside linebacker moves into a nose position directly over the middle guard) and three linebackers stacked directly over the three down defenders. The two defensive tackles line up in a "43" alignment (on the inside shoulder of the offensive tackle—Diagram 9-2), normally play a "4" alignment (head up on the defensive tackle—Diagram 9-3), or in a "3" gap alignment (in the gap between the offensive guard and tackle—Diagram 9-4).

We have found this Fifty-three Triple Stack Defense an excellent stunting defense when we really wanted to go after the offense and shoot our defenders into the opposition's backfield, causing minus yardage, fumbles, and generally confusing the offensive running and passing at-

FIFTY-THREE STACK DEFENSE RESPONSIBILITY CHART

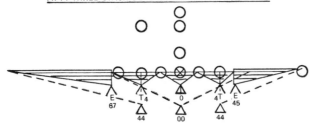

	ALIGNMENT	KEYS BY PROGRESSION	RESPONSIBILITY
ENDS	67	(1) End (2) Near Back (3) Fullback	End to sidelines
TACKLES	4	(1) Tackle (2) Guard (3) End	Nose of guard to nose of end
MIDDLE-GUARD	0	(1) Center (2) Guards (3) Flow of backs	Nose of guard to nose of other guard
LEFT AND RIGHT LINEBACKERS	44	(1) Guard (2) End (3) Near Back	Tackle to sideline
MIDDLE LINEBACKER	00	(1) Flow of backs (2) Guards	End to end

DIAGRAM 9-1a

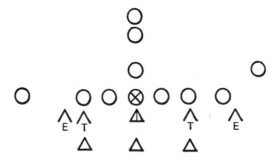

DIAGRAM 9-1b

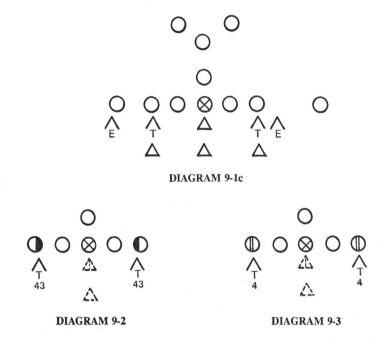

DIAGRAM 9-1c

DIAGRAM 9-2   **DIAGRAM 9-3**

tack. The normal reading Triple Stack Defense has continually mixed up the opponent's number, man, or word-blocking assignments. This stunting and penetrating defense is particularly strong inside the offensive ends, especially utilizing the stacked or tandemed defenders.

Our defensive staff likes the Fifty-three Stack Defense because it gives our normal even defense (no defender on the center's nose) an odd look and an inside linebacker lined up on the offensive center's nose. This odd defense forces the offensive center to block a man on his nose, freeing the middle linebacker, and is a most successful defensive change-up in our Fifty defensive repertoire.

The defensive tackles are the anchors for the stacked defense. If the opponent attempts to split wide to weaken the defense, we tell our defensive tackles to jump into the "3" gap as illustrated in Diagram 9-4. This forces the offensive tackles to close down their offensive splits so the defensive tackles cannot shoot the gap. The nose defensive lineman is assigned the responsibility of taking away the maximum split by the offensive guard. Most opponents are afraid to try to take maximum splits against the Fifty-three Stacked Defense because of the constant threat of the gaming and stunting stacked defenders.

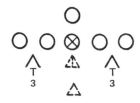

DIAGRAM 9-4

The coaching techniques and alignments of the Fifty-three Stack Defense are:

Nose Man "0." The inside linebacker lines up in an "0" technique, head on the offensive center, and is coached to use a four-point stance. The middle linebacker or nose man is taught to use a forearm or two-hand blast on the center as his initial movement. After the middle man executes his blow, he must fight the pressure of the offensive blocker's pressure, take the correct pursuit course, and make the tackle.

If the play comes the "0" man's way, he must meet blocking power, low and tough and with maximum pressure. The area of his concentration must be from the outside shoulder of both offensive guards. The defender must drop his head and shoulders to get under the potential blockers' heads. He should drop to a four-point defensive stance if the blocker begins to drive him backward. As a last resort, the nose man is taught to use a spin out, only if he is double teamed by the offensive center and guard. He must spin out in the opposite direction of the pressure or the drive man. The first defensive technique we teach to all defensive linemen is to attempt to split the double team by driving the head between the double teaming blockers.

If the opposition runs away from the middle guard, he is taught to fight through the blocker's head and pursue the ball carrier. If the opponent attempts an option play away from the "0" man, he is coached to play the ball from his pursuing position.

As soon as a drop-back or pocket pass shows, the middle defender, playing the "0" technique, is coached to fight through the center's head and then play the middle draw first and the middle screen second. On any drop-back pass play, the "0" man must never be blocked by the offensive center alone. He must deliver his blow on the center and then react to the ball. If a sprint-out pass develops, the middle guard is still responsible for the draw and the screen pass.

Middle Linebacker "00." The "00" man's initial key is the quarterback and fullback. As soon as the ball is put into play, the middle linebacker must be taught to look up the guard to the side the ball is moving, for this is the first uncovered offensive blocker that has a shot at the "00" defender. When the ball carrier attacks the middle area, it is possible for the offense to assign both guards to block the middle linebacker. There is also a strong possibility that the offense may assign the offensive center and play side guard to block the middle linebacker with the offensive tackle. Therefore, the middle linebacker must be ready to scallop toward the ball and be ready for the down block by the offensive tackle. As soon as the middle guard or nose man is double teamed, the middle linebacker must be ready to fill the off-guard hole. The middle linebacker must fill the same hole if the play side or front side guard turns out and blocks the defensive tackle. If both guards pull to one side, the middle guard must flow with the movement of the offensive guards. The flow of the "00" linebacker must be a scalloping shuffle, checking each hole as he moves along with the pulling guards, keeping his shoulders parallel to the line of scrimmage. He must meet the ball carrier head on, with his shoulders square, as soon as the ball carrier cuts upfield. If the ball carrier attacks the middle area, the middle linebacker must attack the ball carrier low and meet blocking pressure with defensive pressure.

When the runner goes away from the middle linebacker, he must be ready to scallop to the point of attack. If the opponent runs an option play, the "00" defender is coached to key and attack the ball. He must be careful never to overrun the ball carrier.

As soon as a drop-back pass shows, the middle linebacker is taught to drop straight back into the middle hook zone. If a sprint-out pass or play action pass shows, the middle linebacker should recognize pass and then take off on a 45 degree angle and play the hook zone to the side of the flow. The reason the middle linebacker is assigned to play the hook zone to the play or front side is that the outside linebacker to the side of the action is taught to attack the sprinting quarterback.

Defensive Tackles "4." The defensive tackles line up nose on the offensive tackles in a "4" technique, using a four-point stance. The tackle is coached to move on the movement of the offensive tackle and deliver a blow on the offensive blocker. The "4" man must key the head of the offensive tackle and deliver a blow with the right or left forearm, depending upon the move of the offensive tackle. The defensive tackle must never be hooked by the offensive blocker or cut off by the blocking tackle. Regardless of the type of block used by the tackle, the defensive tackle must fight pressure of the blocker and fight through the head of the blocking tackle. He must never attempt to run around the block of the offensive tackle because he will never take the proper pursuit course by running "rainbows."

If the ball comes toward the tackle, he must deliver a blow, get rid of the blocker, and make the tackle. The defensive tackle must stay low and drop to all fours whenever he feels the blockers are beginning to drive him out of his position. If the triple option comes his way, he is responsible for closing down and tackling the fullback.

Once the ball goes away from the defensive tackle, he must pursue the ball carrier. If a drop-back pass shows, the tackle should rush, making sure he stays in the correct channel as he takes his all-out rush.

Outside Linebacker "44." The defensive outside linebackers are taught to line up stacked over the defensive tackles, using a balanced two-point stance ("44" technique). The normal depth of the outside linebacker is two yards, but this will vary depending upon the defensive strategy. The outside linebacker is coached to key the near back through the head of the offensive tackle.

If the offensive end attempts to block down upon the stacked outside linebacker, he is taught to meet the offensive end with his outside arm and outside foot. He must deliver a solid blow on the blocker, stepping into the blocker with the same arm, same foot technique. When the outside linebacker is called upon to blitz through the "3" gap (guard-tackle) or the "5" gap (tackle-end), he is taught to dip the near shoulder and be ready to explode through his assigned area. When blitzing, the defensive linebacker should not cheat so close to the line of scrimmage as to give away his blitzing tendencies.

If the ball carrier comes his way, the outside linebacker must take away the off-tackle play first and then help defend the running play to his outside. If the sprint-out option play comes his way, the linebacker normally is assigned to take the quarterback. When the offense runs the triple option maneuver, the linebacker is assigned to stop the fullback (if the defensive tackle takes the quarterback).

If the play goes away, the backside linebacker should first check the counter play and then get into his correct pursuit pattern. The outside linebacker must be coached to scallop deep enough so he is not cut off by a blocker or sprawling football player on his pursuit course. When the sprint-out pass play develops his way, he is taught to attack the sprint out by attacking the quarterback through the "5" gap (tackle-end). If a sprint out develops away, the outside linebacker is assigned to check his hook zone for a potential throw-back pass and then cushion toward the middle of the undercover pass zone.

Defensive Ends "67." The defensive end should line up in a "67" technique, splitting the outside leg of the offensive end with his two feet. The defensive end should use a two-point stance with the inside foot forward and the outside leg back.

The initial move of the "67" defender is to take a quick, short shuffle step with the inside foot and deliver a blow on the offensive end, if the end attempts to block the defensive end. If the offensive end blocks down, the "67" defender should immediately close down to shut off the off-tackle hole. The defensive end normally plays this type of crashing end but may also play a boxing end when lined up in an "8" technique. Whenever the defensive end uses his boxing technique, he is coached to take steps across the line of scrimmage and force or force-contain all plays inside of him. Using the boxing technique places an added responsibility on the outside linebacker to fill and stop the off-tackle play. When the defensive end uses his crashing technique, the outside linebacker should first check the off-tackle hole and then be ready to support the outside sweep, if the opposition sweeps around to the outside of the crashing defensive end.

Basically, the "67" defensive end should take away the sweep and shut off the off-tackle hole if the play goes his way. If the play goes away, the defensive end is coached to chase the play checking for counters, bootlegs, and reverse plays.

On all straight drop-back or pocket passes, the defensive end always uses his contain rush technique.

ADJUSTMENTS TO FORMATIONS FROM THE TRIPLE STACK

Whenever the opposition uses a split end, we basically use our normal stack over the tackle to the short or split end's side. At times we also use our knockdown method, which moves the defensive tackle over the guard and leaves the linebacker stacked behind the defensive tackle (Diagram 9-5), or knock the tackle down to the outside shoulder of the offensive guard. Then we move the previously stacked outside linebacker

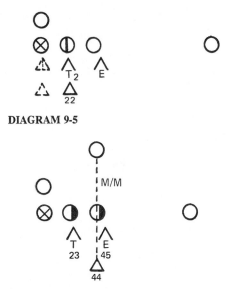

DIAGRAM 9-5

DIAGRAM 9-6

to a head-up position over the offensive tackle in a Revert-type look (Diagram 9-6).

The knockdown stacked is particularly strong against the power "I" formation, as seen in Diagram 9-5. Diagram 9-6 is a strong defense whenever the outside linebacker is in his "44" alignment and is assigned to key the near side back man to man. If we expect a pass on a third and long situation, we may use our third method of knocking down our defenders to the split end's side by using much the same alignment as in Diagram 9-6, but moving the oustide linebacker to his normal "50" and Split Fifty Defense. See Diagram 9-7.

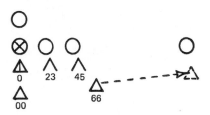

DIAGRAM 9-7

The outside linebacker ("66") in Diagram 9-7 is able to help out quickly on a quick swing pass to the near back and also assist the secondary on curl or look-in pass patterns to the split end. The Fifty-three Triple Stack Defense can also use double coverage on the split end by moving the outside linebacker to the split end's side to a double coverage technique. The defense may chug the split end before he takes off downfield on his pass route.

BLITZING AND STUNTING FROM THE FIFTY-THREE STACK

As stated previously in this chapter, the Fifty-three Stack Defense is an excellent defense to blitz and stunt against the opposition's offense. Numbering our linebackers, we can use the basic Fifty-one Blitz, Fifty-two Blitz, and Fifty-three Blitz Stunts. See Diagrams 9-8, 9-9, and 9-10.

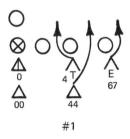

#1

DIAGRAM 9-8
Triple Stack "51 Blitz

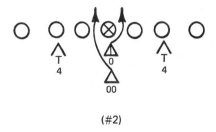

(#2)

DIAGRAM 9-9
Triple Stack "52" Blitz

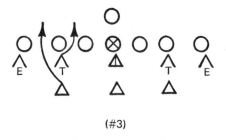

(#3)

DIAGRAM 9-10
Triple Stack "53" Blitz

DIAGRAM 9-11
Triple Stack All vs. 2 T.E.

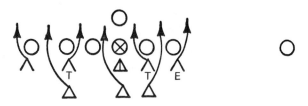

DIAGRAM 9-12
Triple Stack All vs. S.E.

Fifty-three All is illustrated in Diagram 9-11 against two tight ends, and in Diagram 9-12 versus a split end offensive attack.

In Diagram 9-12, the nose man ("0") is coached to play his normal read and position because with a split end attack there are only seven gaps to defend; therefore, there is no gap for the nose man or middle guard to take. He is taught to play his regular assignment and chug the center and then check for the draw or middle screen.

Off the triple stack we can change up the above Fifty-three. Switching the stunts between the left tackle and linebacker, and the right outside linebacker and right tackle, drives the outside right linebacker into the "3" gap and loops the right tackle out and through the "5" gap. See Diagram 9-13. This would be called Fifty-three Triple Switch.

DIAGRAM 9-13
Triple Switch

The Fifty-three Stack Defense is also used as an angling or looping defense. Whenever we want to loop to the strength of the defense or to the wide side of the field, we initiate a loop Ringo (Diagram 9-14).

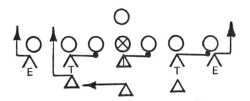

DIAGRAM 9-14
Triple Stack Loop Ringo

After we complete our loop right, we actually end up in a 6-1 or Pro-like look in the middle. This is accomplished by teaching the defensive left tackle to loop head up into the offensive right guard. The technique for the looper is to take a short glide with the front side foot and

then step with the backside foot. The defender is taught to keep his
shoulders parallel to the line of scrimmage and his entire body in a good
hitting football position, in the event the blocker attempts to block him
right now! The middle nose man and the right defensive tackle use the
same type of maneuver as illustrated in Diagram 9-14. The right defensive end is taught to shuffle two steps to his right and then to take two
steps directly upfield. The defensive end now boxes in any potential
sweep that comes his way. The middle linebacker is coached to stay head
up on the center ("00"). The outside left linebacker shuffles quickly to
his left on the snap of the ball, and then shoots directly over the outside
shoulder of the offensive right tackle. The left defensive end uses his
normal "67" technique and attacks into the opponent's backfield directly
over the outside shoulder of the offensive right end's position (Diagram
9-15).

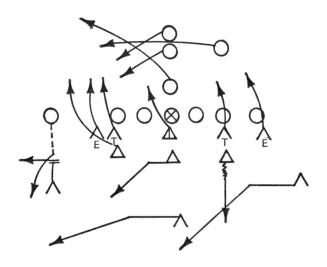

DIAGRAM 9-15

10

The Three-Deep Pass Defense

The defensive eight-man fronts, like the Fifty Monster Defense, Fifty-three, Fifty-three Stack, and others, have greatly increased the interest in the three-deep locked-in zone (no rotation), the revolving zone, and three-deep man-to-man pass defense. The objective of the three-deep zone pass defense is to stay as deep as the deepest receiver and as wide as the widest receiver.

While the eight-man front defensive teams are basically zone pass defenses, there are times when the three-deep secondary will play man-to-man coverage underneath (defensive linebackers), three-deep man-to-man in the secondary, or a combination of zone and man-to-man pass defense. Combine these secondaries and underneath coverages with a strong rush or holding-up potential pass receivers, and this secondary offers a varied assortment for defending against the pass.

COACHING PASS DEFENSE

An outstanding pass defender has poise and the confidence that he can make the big play in a clutch situation. He must have a burning desire to make an interception whenever the opposition puts the ball into the air.

All of our pass defenders are coached to communicate with each other continually just prior to the snap of the ball, as well as while the ball is in play. The outstanding pass defender continually practices to improve his reaction time and constantly works on his pass coverage technique and on sprinting back to his target areas.

The pass defender must learn to read his key, and if a zone coverage pattern has been called, he must keep his eyes on the passer zone call.

This will allow the defender to get a jump on the pass and cover more ground in an attempt to intercept the ball. When it is impossible to make the interception, a proper pursuit course may cut off the long run. The pass defender must believe in the pass defense. Therefore, all of our secondary defenders must know their proper pursuit course versus the run as well as the pass. If the pass receiver makes the catch in the pass defender's area, the pass receiver will be forced to drop the ball. If the receiver makes a catch in a particular zone, we expect the pass defender in that zone to make up for his mistake by making an interception on the next pass in his zone. We want our secondary so confident that they hope the opposition will put the ball in the air, because once the ball is in the air, "It is ours!"

DEFENSIVE SECONDARY COACHING POINTS

The defensive secondary does not run a defensive pass drill without using live receivers. As soon as the passer throws the ball, the defensive secondary and linebackers are coached to yell "Ball!" As soon as a defender intercepts a pass, he is coached to yell "Bingo!" This puts the entire defense on the offense and alerts the interceptor's teammates to block. When intercepting the ball, the defender is taught to go through the receiver's head, look the ball into his hands, and catch the ball at its highest point.

During practice sessions the defensive backs use both oral and hand signals to call the pass defense. All defensive secondary members are taught to communicate at all times with one another. If the demonstration team, in practice, completes a bomb against the defense, all the secondary and linebackers are coached to chase the receiver into the end zone and touch him.

COMPLETED PASS—DON'T PANIC

The defensive coordinator must sell the principle that the opposition will complete certain passes whether we are in a zone, man to man, or a combination of these two—but don't panic! The defensive unit must be taught the weak points as well as the strong points of all pass defenses. The change-up pass coverages, plus a combination of blitzes and odd and even rushing techniques, will help to force the offensive passing attack into a number of mistakes. The coaches must stress the importance of the defense being in the proper place at the right time, and they will force the opposition into interceptions, fumbles, and missed assignments.

COACHING HOW TO TEACH BACK-PEDALLING TO DEFENDERS

Of prime importance to pass defenders is back-pedalling, which enables them to move backward while keeping the potential receiver and passer in full view. In teaching this defensive technique, the coach must be sure the defender bends his body, drops his hips, and hugs his feet close to the ground (drag steps) as he retreats from the line of scrimmage.

The runner should drop back by running on the balls of his feet. His arms should pump like pistons, enabling him to gain speed and stay on balance. Short steps should be used by the pass defender and his knees must be flexed. He should have a solid base so that he will be able to react to any inside or outside move by the pass receiver.

Once the defender has lost his required cushion on the potential receiver, he is coached to turn and run directly for the potential receiver as quickly as possible. Then he is coached to watch the potential receiver's eyes. As soon as the eyes enlarge, signaling that the ball is about to be caught, the defender should throw up his arms in front of the potential receiver's eyes.

INTERCEPTING THE BALL

The defender should go for the ball, taking the shortest and most direct route. The secondary defender should go for the interception at the highest point, extending his arms and twisting his hips toward the intended receiver. Just before he makes the interception, he should shout "Bingo!" to alert all of his teammates that he is attempting to make the interception. This call also alerts the other pass defenders to be ready to block for the interceptor or react to a tipped or batted ball. As soon as the interception is made, the defender should break for the sidelines and sprint for the goal line.

STRIPPING THE INTENDED RECEIVER

If the defensive back cannot get to the pass receiver in time to make the interception, he should put his shoulder into the intended receiver's target and knock the receiver loose from the ball. As soon as the shoulder reaches the target, the defender should bring his arms upward or downward to attempt to knock the ball loose by stripping the potential receiver of the ball.

SECONDARY BLOCK PROTECTION

One important phase of coaching the defensive secondary is coaching the defender on how to defeat a downfield block. The coaching points in getting rid of the blocker must emphasize coming up under control with the defender's shoulders parallel to the line of scrimmage so he can fight off the block and make the tackle.

If the blocker uses a low rolling or chopping block, the defensive back must use his arms and hands to ward off the blocker, making sure the blocker does not get into his legs. We tell our defenders, "Use your muscles (arms and hands) to keep the blocker off your wheels (legs)."

If the blocker uses a snoot or high number block, we teach the defender to ward off the blocker with his forearm and get rid of the blocker with his other hand. This is usually used by the cornerback when he uses his force-contain squeeze-like technique to turn the sweep to the inside.

The deep defender must defeat the block and force the ball carrier to cut inside. This will turn the ball carrier inside into the defensive pursuing unit. If the ball carrier breaks outside, the defender must come off the block and *he* must make the tackle.

When the defensive secondary back recognizes the play is a run, he must attack the ball carrier on or near the line of scrimmage. The defender should take on the blocker at the line of scrimmage, using the same arm, same leg block protection technique. The defender should defeat the blocker and make sure he stays beaten (does not roll up into the defender's legs). The defender must use his shoulder or forearm if the blocker attempts to snoot block the defender in the numbers.

SECONDARY STANCE (THREE DEEP)

The defensive cornerbacks should assume a good balanced football position just prior to the snap of the ball. The defenders should flex their knees with the outside foot back in a heel-toe relationship. The arms should hang down freely inside the knees.

Whenever the cornerbacks are assigned to defend the potential receiver in a man-to-man assignment, the defender is coached to use a more parallel stance, maintaining equal balance between the two feet.

The defensive safetyman uses a more parallel stance when assigned to a zone pass defense because he may move quickly in any direction, depending upon the offensive maneuver. His knees should be flexed slightly, with the weight on the balls of his feet. His arms should hang down freely just inside his knees.

THREE-DEEP SECONDARY ALIGNMENT FOR THE SAFETYMAN

Safety Alignment:

1. Line up eleven or twelve yards deep over either offensive guard, depending upon position between hash marks (Diagram 10-1).
2. Never line up closer than two yards inside the hash mark (Diagram 10-2).

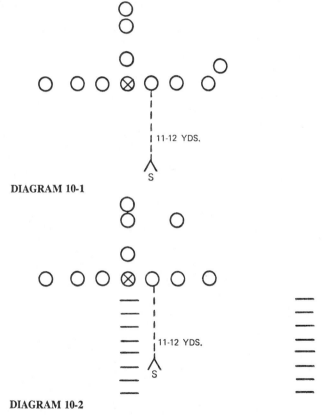

DIAGRAM 10-1

DIAGRAM 10-2

3. If the ball is in the middle of the field, the safety should line up over the guard to the two quickest receivers or top receivers.

Safety: Key the ball, then check strong side receivers (Diagrams 10-3 and -4).

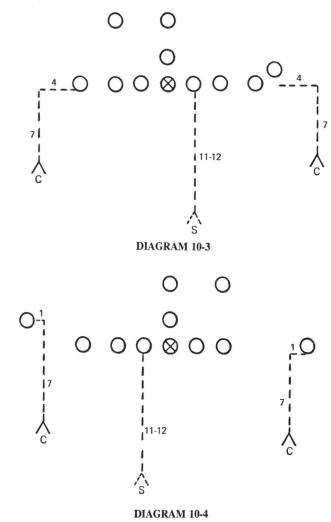

DIAGRAM 10-3

DIAGRAM 10-4

SAFETY

Drop-Back Pass. The safety should take a quick jab step backward and take a picture of the play. If drop-back pass shows, he should drop straight back for the deep middle target area. Key the quarterback at all times. Watch the quarterback's feet, and then react to the passer's shoulders which will indicate the direction of the pass. Once the ball has been passed, take the shortest and most direct route possible to the ball.

Sprint Pass. Take a short read step back and sprint for the target area, getting width and depth to reach the deep outside one-third area as soon as possible. If two receivers are in the deep outside one-third zone, cover the deepest and widest receiver in the outside one-third zone.

Support the Run. Take a short step back and then support the sweep from an inside-out angle, coming up inside the cornerback's force-contain position. If the ball gets outside the cornerback's position, the safety must take a proper flat angle to the sidelines to cut the ball off. If the ball carrier runs up the middle or cuts off tackle, the safetyman should come under control and keep his shoulders square to the line of scrimmage as he attacks the ball carrier.

THREE-DEEP SECONDARY ALIGNMENT FOR CORNERS

Corner's Alignment:

1. Versus Tight End—Seven yards deep, four yards outside (Diagrams 10-5 and 10-6).

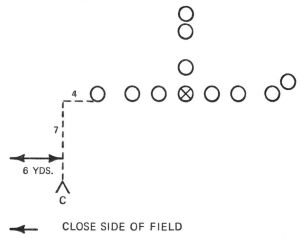

DIAGRAM 10-5

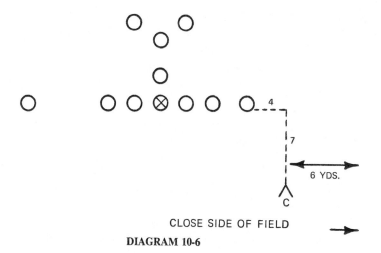

CLOSE SIDE OF FIELD

DIAGRAM 10-6

2. Versus Tight Wing—Seven yards deep, four yards outside.
3. Versus Tight End/Wing—Up to four yards split, stay outside shoulder seven yards deep.
4. Versus Tight End/Wing—Seven yards or more split, one yard inside seven yards deep (Diagram 10-7).
5. Never line up closer than six yards from sidelines (Diagrams 10-5 and 10-6).
6. Never line up further than fifteen yards from safety (Diagram 10-7).

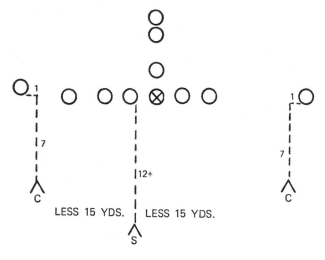

DIAGRAM 10-7

Corners: Key the ball first, then wing back or end to your side.

Coaching Note: If the Fifty Monster Defense is used, the corner-back (halfback) away from the monster will normally move up as close as five yards deep. The other two deep defenders will also move up closer to the line of scrimmage, depending upon down, distance, etc.

CORNERBACK (HALFBACK)

Drop-Back Pass. The defender should take a short read step back and to the outside and take a picture of the play. As soon as he reads drop-back pass, he should sprint for lateral depth and width. He should shoot for the middle of his target area and never get closer than six yards to the sidelines.

Sprint Pass To. Take a quick step backward to the outside and read the action. As the quarterback sprints toward the cornerman, he should sprint for the target area and maintain an outside-in position on the ball. Keep the receiver in your zone (three yards) on your inside shoulder. Hang and then level off at seven yards deep or sprint back for the deep outside one-third target zone.

Sprint Pass Away. Take a quick step back with the outside foot and read sprint-away action. Sprint back for deep outside one-third target area, on a freeze, or begin to roll to cover the deep two-thirds zone. Keep the potential receiver on the inside shoulder. Check the near side halfback for a possible throw-back pass, if two receivers in the zone play the deepest threat.

Run Support To. Take a quick step back with the outside foot and support the run from an outside-in angle. The defender should come under control, keep his shoulders parallel to the line of scrimmage, and force-contain the sweep from an outside-in angle. Meet the lead blocker as tough and tight as possible. He should not go so deep that the blocker can turn the defender outside. This would open up a funnel for the ball carrier. The defender should give ground grudgingly, and get rid of the blocker as soon as possible.

WATCH THE BALL

All three-deep secondary defenders in the zone pass defense must defend against the ball. If the quarterback drops straight back in a pocket in the middle of the field, the defenders should start their drops on a 45 degree angle with the middle safetyman dropping off into his middle one-third zone. The three pass defenders should never be more than fifteen yards apart, because any greater width would open up too wide a seam between the safetyman and the cornerman. The deep defenders are coached to drop back as deep as the deepest man in their zone and as wide as the widest potential receiver in their assigned area.

If Cover One (Diagrams 10-8, 10-9, and 10-10) or Cover Two (Diagrams 10-11, 10-12, and 10-13) is called, the defenders responsible for the deep one-third or two-thirds zones must get vertical and lateral depth as quickly as possible. As soon as the ball goes away, the cornerman assigned the deep two-thirds zone must gain depth, looking for the possible throw-back first and lateral movement second. The two-thirds defender should revolve through the safetyman's position.

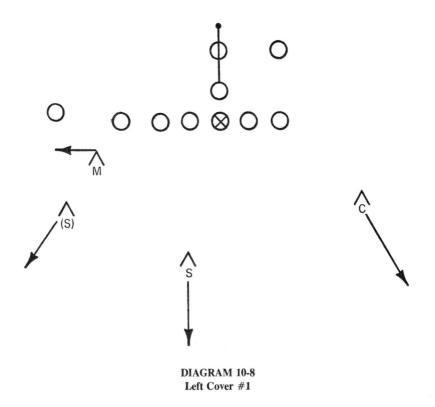

DIAGRAM 10-8
Left Cover #1

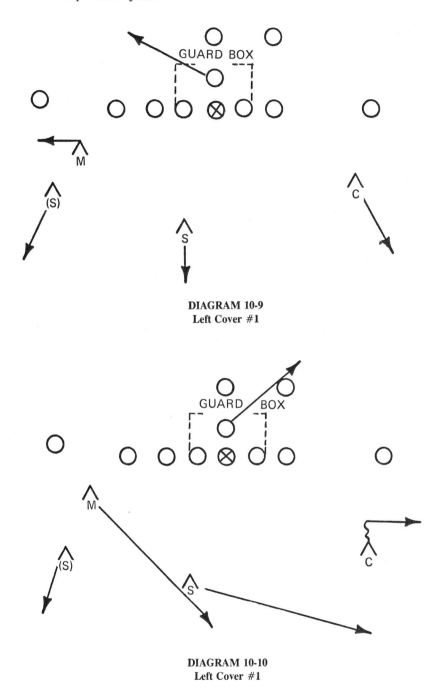

DIAGRAM 10-9
Left Cover #1

DIAGRAM 10-10
Left Cover #1

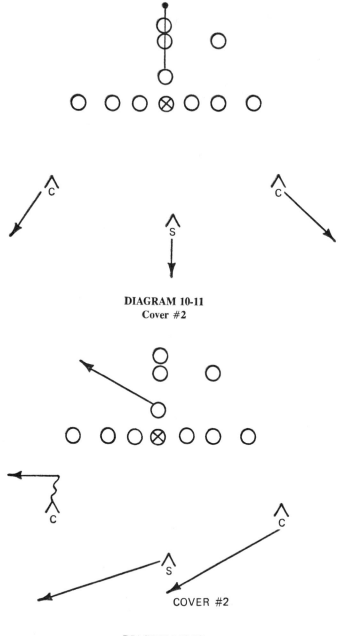

DIAGRAM 10-11
Cover #2

COVER #2

DIAGRAM 10-12
Cover #2

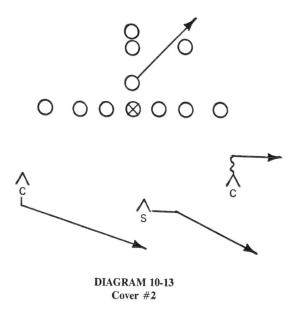

DIAGRAM 10-13
Cover #2

COVERAGE ANGLE (ZONE)

As stated previously, the secondary defenders drop off at 45 degree angles as long as the ball is in the middle of the field, maintaining a three-by-three yard relationship on the potential receiver in his zone. The three-by-three relationship consists of a three-yard cushion laterally and a three-yard zone cushion vertically.

If the deep defender is covering an area between the hash mark and the six-yard imaginary line from the sideline, he should drop back more on a straight line since the width of the assigned zone has been lessened.

THREE-DEEP CALLS

The middle safetyman calls the secondary coverage calls to his fellow secondary and linebacker teammates. The coverage calls are based upon the offensive formation, lateral-vertical field position, score, down-distance relationship, and time left in the game. The middle safetyman in the three-deep secondary may call one of four coverage calls: Cover One, Cover Two, Cover Three (and Cover Twenty-three, which is a combination of Two and Three coverage), and Man-to-Man.

All of the former coverage calls are zone, with the last the only man-to-man assignment.

LEFT COVER #1 (Diagrams 10-8, 10-9, and 10-10)

Monster (Strong)

Stance: See stance.

Alignment: Use walk-away position three yards deep and split the difference between the wide receiver and the next eligible receiver.

Responsibility:

Sprint To: Cover the flat.

Sprint Away: Sprint to the deep middle one-third zone and replace the revolving safetyman who has sprinted to the playside deep one-third zone.

Drop Back: Cover the flat.

Left Cornerman

Stance: See stance.

Alignment: See alignment.

Responsibility:

Sprint To: Drop outside one-third zone.
Sprint Away: Drop outside one-third zone.
Drop Back: Drop outside one-third zone.

Safetyman

Stance: See stance.

Alignment: See alignment.

Responsibility:

Sprint To (left): Deep middle one-third zone.

Sprint Away (right): Safetyman revolves to defend the deep outside one-third zone to the side of the sprint-out passer. The safetyman must gain width and then depth to his zone and then play the ball. The safetyman revolves as soon as as the quarterback sprints outside of the guard box. The safety is able to revolve in only one direction, away from the call or strong side (Diagram 10-10).

Drop Back: Deep middle one-third zone.

Right Cornerman

Stance: See stance.

Alignment: See alignment.

Responsibility:

Sprint To: Safetyman yells "Rotation!" as soon as the sprint-out passer sprints outside the guard box. The right cornerman should shuffle back or hang until he hears the call. He then charges the receiver and steps up and lands off the outside to defend the flat zone to his side.

Drop Back: Cover the deep outside one-third zone.

Sprint Away: Cover the deep outside one-third zone.

Coaching Note: The defensive safetyman must warn the monster man rover back to be ready to cover the deep middle one-third zone as soon as the ball goes away from his position. Once the ball has broken the guard box, all the deep defenders must be coached to call "Sprint right!" This reminds the strong side linebacker or rover to cover the deep middle one-third and tells the right cornerman to hang, then attack the flat zone to his side. If the right cornerback is in doubt, he should hang and cover the deep outside zone. It is far better to have two deep secondary defenders in the deep outside one-third zone and none in the flat, than not to have anyone defend the deep outside one-third zone.

COVER #2 (Diagrams 10-11, 10-12, and 10-13)

Cover #2 is called, which allows the safetyman to revolve in either the left or the right direction. If a straight drop-back pass shows, the three-deep defenders cover their respective deep one-third zones. Both the cornermen have the assignments to level off into the flats if the ball comes their way or cover the deep two-thirds if the ball goes away from their positions.

Cornerbacks

Stance: See stance.

Alignment: See alignment.

Responsibility:

Sprint To: Hang and then chug the potential receiver. Level off and cover the flat zone to the ball side. Remember—do not chug and level off until the ball breaks the guard box.

Drop Back: Cover the deep outside one-third zone.

Sprint Away: As soon as the ball goes away and breaks the guard box, gain depth first and width next, and cover the deep two-thirds zone.

Safetyman

Stance: See stance.

Alignment: See alignment.

Responsibility:

Sprint To and Sprint Away: Revolve in either direction and cover the deep outside one-third zone, keying the ball.

Drop Back: Cover the deep middle one-third zone.

Coaching Note: Whenever the offensive formation splits two wide receivers, in opposite directions, so widely that it is impossible to use a Cover #2 call, the middle safetyman is coached to use a Cover #3 call. This call locks the three defenders into their deep one-third zones, regardless of what direction the ball moves in.

COVER #3 (Diagram 10-14)

Cornerbacks

Stance: See stance.

Alignment: See alignment.

Responsibility:

Sprint To, Drop Back, and Sprint Away: Cover the assigned deep outside one-third zone regardless of the direction of the ball.

Safetyman

Stance: See stance.

Alignment: See alignment.

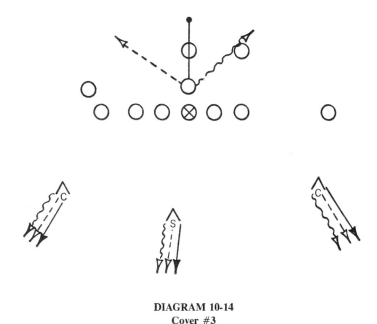

DIAGRAM 10-14
Cover #3

Responsibility:

Sprint To, Drop Back, and Sprint Away: Cover the deep middle one-third zone regardless of the direction of the ball.

Coaching Note: The Cover #3 Call locks all three of the secondary defenders in a three-deep zone alignment regardless of the direction of the ball. The Cover #3 Call is used against an expected passing down when the opposition uses two wide potential receivers in opposite directions. This three-deep locked-in zone is also used as a victory defense late in a contest when the offense is forced to go for the bomb. The #3 Call is our simplest and often our most effective pass coverage call (Diagram (10-14).

COVER #23 WEAK (Diagrams 10-15, 10-16, and 10-17)

Cover #23 Weak is a combination of Cover #2 and Cover #3. The word "weak" signifies that we will use the Cover #2 level only to the weak side (Diagram 10-15). If the ball drops straight back or goes to the

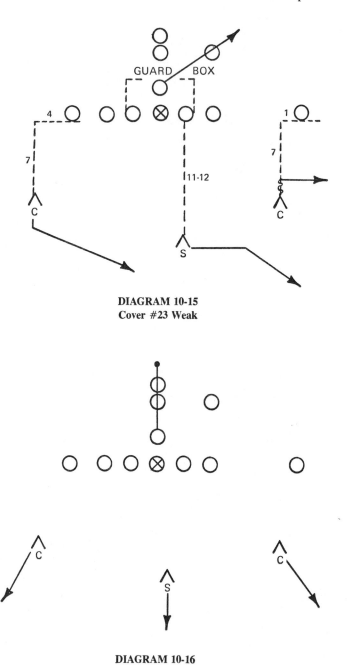

DIAGRAM 10-15
Cover #23 Weak

DIAGRAM 10-16
Cover #23

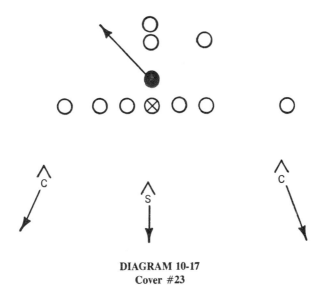

DIAGRAM 10-17
Cover #23

defensive left, the pass defensive secondary defenders simply stay in their normal locked-in three-deep non-revolving defense.

Right Corner

Stance: Outside foot back with the weight on the forward foot. Shoulders should be parallel. Normal football position with hips dropped slightly and arms dangling just below the knees.

Alignment: On any possible Rip or rotation calls, line up one yard inside and seven yards deep on the wide split receiver.

Key: Key eligible potential receiver (split end) and then flow. Listen for safety's rotation call.

1. *Coverage–Flow To:* Revolve up cautiously, forcing all receivers inside. Chug the receiver if he comes your way, but don't move inside to go after him. If pass shows, move to the outside flat about seven yards deep and look for the first potential receiver to enter the zone. Play this potential receiver tight. If pass still shows and no potential receiver enters the zone, drop back deep and don't just "cover air." If run comes, revolve up and force-contain the ball carrier to the inside so pursuit will attack the ball carrier. Meet all blockers with the shoulders parallel to the goal line and meet the

first blocker with the inside forearm and inside leg. Remember, squeeze the play to the inside. If in doubt to rotate, *stay deep!*

2. *Coverage–Flow Away:* Drop back deep and cover the deep outside one-third area as the pass defense is in a three-deep freeze coverage technique.

3. *Coverage–Back-up Pass:* Drop back into deep one-third outside zone and play the ball.

Left Corner

Stance: Same as right cornerback.

Alignment: Four yards outside of the tight end and seven yards deep.

Key: Key eligible potential receiver (tight end) and then key flow. Listen for safety's rotation call.

1. *Cover Flow to Play:* Cover deep one-third zone until sure it is a run, and then force-contain the sweep.

2. *Coverage–Flow Away:* Revolve, gaining depth first and width second. Responsible to cover two-thirds of the field and look for the possible throw-back pass.

3. *Coverage–Back-up Pass:* Drop back into deep one-third outside zone and play the ball.

Safety

Stance: Two-point parallel stance with the shoulders parallel to the line of scrimmage. The weight should be distributed on the balls of the feet. The arms should dangle freely inside and just below the knees.

Alignment: Line up eleven to twelve yards deep directly over the offensive guard to the side of the two quickest receivers (strong side offensive guard).

Key: Key the ball and make a rotation call as soon as the ball crosses outside of the scrimmage guard box. (Example, ''Sprint Right.'')

1. *Coverage Flow (Split Side):* As soon as the ball crosses the outside of the imaginary guard box, the safety should make his call while he is gaining width first and depth second. The safety should get to the hash mark to the flow side, about twenty yards deep as a basic rule.

He must be able to cover the deepest and the widest receiver in the one-third deep zone.

2. *Coverage Flow To (Tight End Side) or Drop Straight Back Pass:* Cover the deep one-third middle zone.

THREE-DEEP MAN-TO-MAN PASS DEFENSE

To help confuse the offensive quarterback, we also use a three-deep man-to-man pass defense off our regular three-deep look. We simply move one deep safetyman over slightly to play the tight end in a man-to-man assignment. The two cornerbacks play the two wide receivers in the same manner (Diagram 10-18).

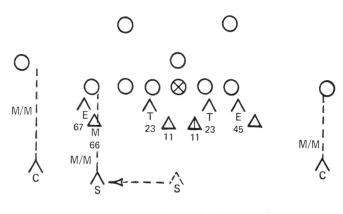

DIAGRAM 10-18
Three-Deep Man-to-Man

ADJUSTING TO A SPLIT FIFTY DEFENSE

When moving from a normal Fifty Defense to a Split Fifty Look, we leave our whole right knockdown side with the same personnel and alignment as we use in our normal Fifty Knockdown. We then simply slide our strong tackle and strong linebacker down one man and move the monster to a head-up "66" position (Diagram 10-18).

If the offense lines up with two tight ends, we use the same alignment and the same defenders in their same positions. The defense remains a five-man line with three linebackers and a three-deep secondary pass defense.

The secondary moves to their three-deep alignment, moving the left safetyman to the monster's side (Diagram 10-19).

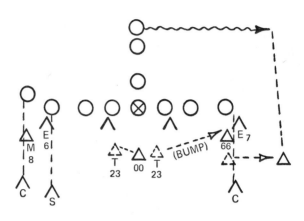

DIAGRAM 10-19
Adjust to Man-to-Man

The strong inside split linebacker and the monster, to the tight end, play inside-outside on the strong side running back. The weak inside split linebacker, middle guard, and the weakside linebacker play inside-outside on the weakside running back also (Diagram 10-19).

The middle safety would drop back and play the tight end man to man, and the right corner would drift out and play the motion back in a man-to-man technique.

MOTION ADJUSTMENT FROM THE THREE-DEEP SECONDARY

Motion adjustment from the three-deep secondary is taken care of by the linebackers. The signal calling linebacker directs the slide of the linebackers. Motion versus the tight Split Fifty Defense usually turns the defense into a normal Monster Defense.

Diagram 10-20 illustrates the monster sliding toward motion which puts the secondary into a Three Call. This call freezes or locks the deep defenders into their respective three-deep zones regardless of the direction

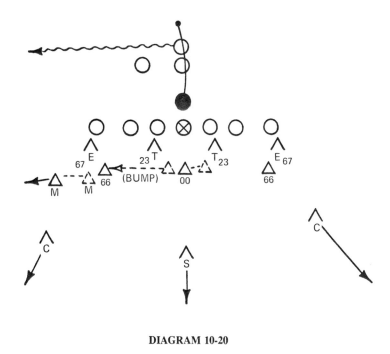

DIAGRAM 10-20

of the passer. The linebacker movement (Diagram 10-20) changes the Split Fifty look to a Fifty-three Middle Look.

DEFENSING THE SPRINT-OUT PASS

To effectively rush a sprint-out pass, the defense must rush at least six men. It is impossible to force an interception consistently versus a sprint-out pass with only four defenders rushing the sprint pass action. Along with the six-man rush against the sprint action, the defense must also place a defender in the flat as well as placing one deep secondary pass defender in the deep outside one-third area in the direction of the sprinting quarterback. Usually the six-man rush will force the quarterback to throw a bad pass, and this gives the defensive secondary a greater interception possibility.

Therefore, we like to use our Fire Stunt off our Split Fifty Defense. The Fire Stunt tells the inside linebacker away from the sprint to fire through an opening and attack the quarterback from a backside or blind angle. If the firing linebacker is unable to find an opening, he is coached to scallop backward and continue his scalloping along the line of scrimmage. The frontside linebacker reads the quarterback's action and then drops back on an angle to defend against the potential ·pass, but also heading in the proper direction to cut off the quarterback if he attempts to run. Both defensive ends rush, using their force-contain rushing techniques. The monster man also puts on an outside-in rush which gives the defense a six-man rush (Diagram 10-21).

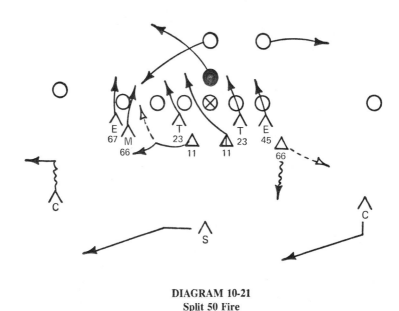

DIAGRAM 10-21
Split 50 Fire

The frontside flat is defended against by the playside defensive left corner who collisions the widest receiver and then plays the flat area. The middle safetyman is assigned the deep one-third defensive pass coverage area, while the offside cornerback is coached to defend the deep two-thirds pass area. The backside weak linebacker then is taught to drop or shuffle back and then get into his proper rotation pattern (Diagram 10-21).

UNDERNEATH COVERAGE (ZONE)

The maximum underneath coverage consists of four linebackers in

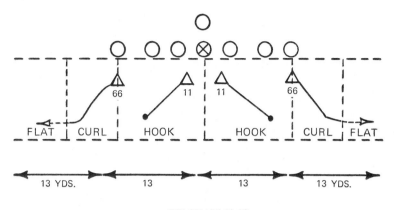

DIAGRAM 10-22
Underneath Coverage

the Split Fifty Defense (Diagram 10-22). The underneath area is actually divided into six zones (2 flat, 2 hook, and 2 curl) because of the increasingly common use of the curl zones (Diagram 10-24).

These underneath defenders must be coached to play their zone or area first and then react to the ball, once it is in the air. The defender must get to the middle of his assigned areas and reach to the ball and not try to cover a specific man in his area. The outstanding zone defender quickly learns to react to the passer's feet position and throwing arm, to get an added "jump" on the ball. Quickness, lateral movement, agility, "soft" hands, and peripheral vision are all important qualities a coach looks for in selecting an underneath defender.

Each underneath defender is responsible for defending an approximate thirteen-yard area (Diagram 10-23). Once the defender occupies the

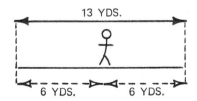

DIAGRAM 10-23
Linebacker's Area

middle of this area, he has only six yards to cover to either his right or his left, because his body occupies about one yard (Diagram 10-23).

SIX UNDERNEATH ZONES

The defensive zones are illustrated with the six short zones and the three deep zones. The reason we use six instead of four short zones is the increasingly common use of the curl zones (Diagram 10-24).

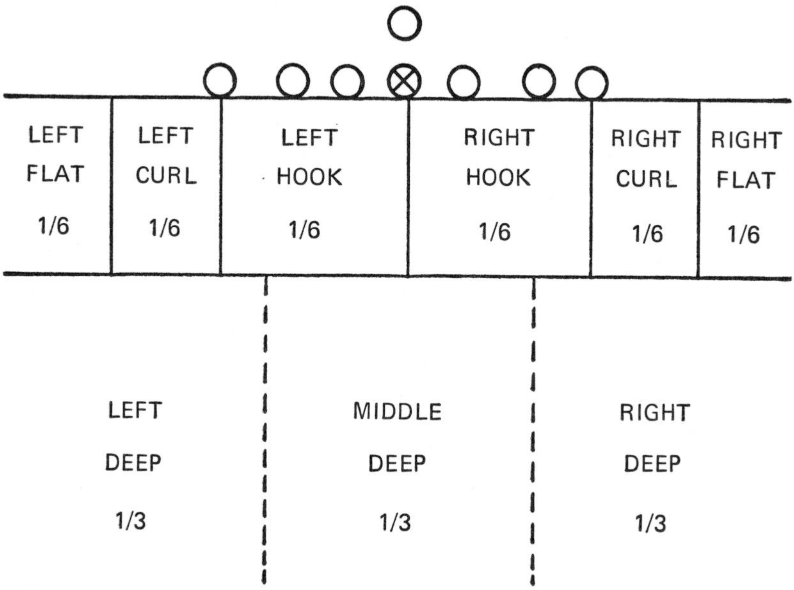

LEFT FLAT 1/6	LEFT CURL 1/6	LEFT HOOK 1/6	RIGHT HOOK 1/6	RIGHT CURL 1/6	RIGHT FLAT 1/6

LEFT DEEP 1/3	MIDDLE DEEP 1/3	RIGHT DEEP 1/3

DIAGRAM 10-24

The flat zones are located eight yards outside the original position of the tight end to a depth of ten yards from the line of scrimmage. The curl zones have the same areas but are used more exclusively in the seams between the flat and the hook zones. The hook zones go from the area of the original position of the tight end to the center and ten yards in depth from the line of scrimmage. The left deep zone goes from the hash mark to the sidelines in width and to the goal line in depth. The middle safety zone stretches from hash mark to hash mark in width and to the goal line in depth.

Coaching Note: Defensive zones are designed with the ball in the direct middle of the field.

LINEBACKERS' TARGET ZONES

Whenever the three-deep freeze call is on, all three of the deep secondary defenders stay in their deep three zones regardless of whether the quarterback drops straight back or sprints or rolls out in either direction. Therefore, the linebackers must be ready to move out quickly and defend the flat and curl zones to the side of the sprint or roll-out action. The speed with which the linebackers move depends upon the speed of the sprint or roll-out action. Therefore, the linebackers' zones move as the passer sprints out. The farther the passer sprints away from the backside outside linebacker, the straighter a drop-back angle the outside linebacker may use.

Therefore, if the moving quarterback moves from the hash mark past the middle of the field, the linebackers' target zones would also continue to move. The linebacker's speed and distance depend upon the speed and lateral movement of the ball. As soon as the action pass lateral movement stops, the linebacker's lateral movement should also stop and then the linebackers should get depth (Diagrams 10-25, 10-26, and 10-27).

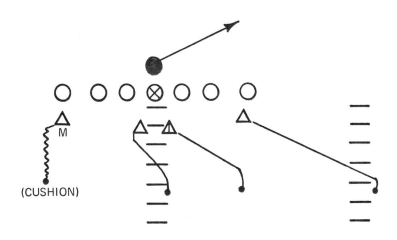

DIAGRAM 10-25

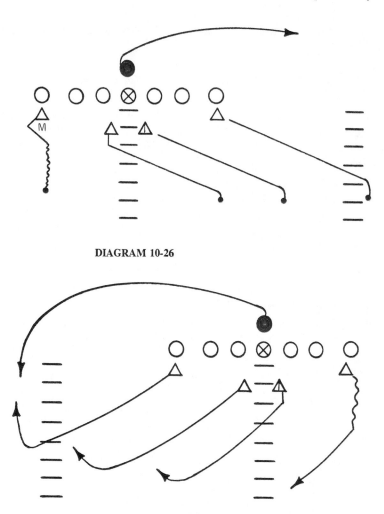

DIAGRAM 10-26

DIAGRAM 10-27

LINEBACKER'S PASS DEFENSE:

Drop-Back Pass Angle: As soon as the linebacker reads the pass, he should drop back to his target area, and then his second step should be a crossover step with the other foot. As he uses his crossover step, he should rotate his hips so that he can look over his shoulder closest to the line of scrimmage. As he drops back, he should check the passer's footwork, as the passer's feet will point out the direction of the pass. As soon as the passer sets up, the linebacker should set up and keep his feet moving so he is able to break in the direction of the pass. The linebacker's head should swivel so that he can check for the possible draw, screen, or an opposition's potential receiver breaking into the area. If the potential receiver breaks into the linebacker's area before the pass is thrown, the linebacker is coached to hook or knock the potential receiver down. The linebacker must keep his feet under his body and not use steps so long that he will be unable to reach in any direction.

Passer Sets Up—Linebacker Sets Up: When the linebacker reads the passer setting up, the linebacker sets up with his shoulders parallel to the line of scrimmage. The defender should set up with his weight balanced and his feet no wider than twelve to fifteen inches. The linebacker should move on the passer's first arm movement, whether it be a fake or an actual pass. Not too many high school or college passers can or have time to arm fake or "look off" a pass and then throw in another direction. One of the best methods the defender has for an interception is to break in front of the intended receiver and make the interception. Therefore, we make sure our linebackers do a lot of reading the passer's shoulders and footwork.

Go for the Ball—Now! All pass defenders are taught to sprint to the area where the passer throws the ball. Our defenders are always taught to think "interception," but, if they are too late to intercept the ball, they may be able to make a block following an interception or make the tackle. On all short passes, it is imperative that the linebacker make his move to intersect the flight of the pass after the ball is in the air. If the linebacker is in front of the intended receiver while the passer has the ball, chances are that the passer will throw the ball to an open receiver.

Intercepting the Pass: The linebacker should always attempt to intercept the pass with his hands. The defender must have "soft" hands, or hands that will give with a bullet or fast pass. This is especially true of the defender who is moving fast toward the passer. The defender should get his body directly in front of the pass; in the event the ball passes through his hands, it will hit his body. The defender should always attack or go for the ball rather than wait for the ball. If he waits for the ball, the receiver may outrun him for the ball or suddenly cut in front of the waiting defender and make the catch.

Stripping the Receiver: If it is impossible to make the interception, the linebacker should strip the intended receiver by butting him with his helmet and then bring his arms upward in an attempt to knock the ball loose from the receiver. Stripping is only used when the defender arrives too late or is in a poor position to make the interception.

Linebacker's Drop Targets: These are illustrated in Diagrams 10-28, 10-29, and 10-30.

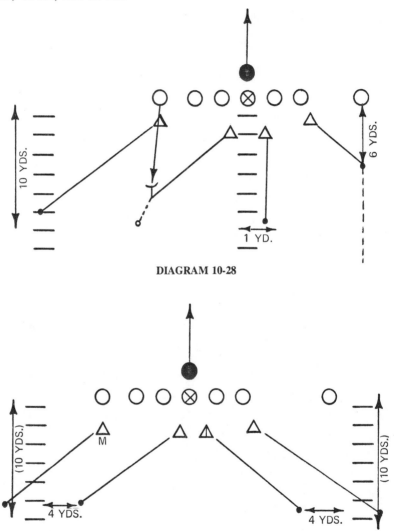

DIAGRAM 10-28

DIAGRAM 10-29

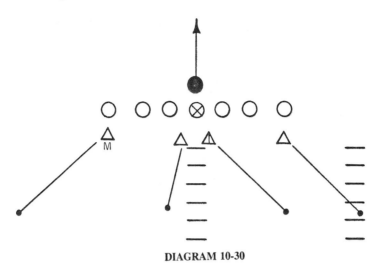

DIAGRAM 10-30

Coaching Points: All linebackers should make "pass," "ball," or "Ringo" calls. Right linebacker (middle guard) should always check for draws. Outside linebackers should look for screens, call screen and react to it. Once linebackers reach target drop areas, they keep their heads swiveling and knock down any crossing receivers before the ball is in the air.

Defensive Outside Cornerman: The basic pass defense is the three-deep locked-in zone pass defense. This means the three-deep pass defenders are assigned a deep secondary zone for which they are responsible on all pass plays, whether the quarterback drops straight back into his pocket, sprints out, or throws a play-action pass.

The deep outside cornerman is coached to line up about two yards outside the offensive end or widest potential receiver and from six to eight yards deep. He uses a two-point stance, with the outside foot slightly back so that he can drop off to his outside one-third zone as soon as a pass develops. The deep outside pass defender is taught to key the outside receiver and play pass first and run second. As soon as the ball is snapped, the wide cornerman is coached to take a quick picture of the play and then shift his weight to the outside foot and push off with his inside foot.

If the end or the wide key blocks, the outside cornerman is coached to attack the ball carrier, using an outside-in angle. As soon as his key releases off the line of scrimmage, the deep middle safetyman must drop back into his deep outside one-third area. The deep cornerman cannot come up too soon just because his key blocks, for the backside receiver may cut across the field and run a pass pattern deep into the vacated deep one-third zone. All cornermen are coached to drop back as deep as the deepest receiver and, basically, as wide as the widest receiver. An exception to this rule is the six-yard zone from the sidelines that the deep defender is taught never to enter until the ball has been put into the air.

If a running play comes in the deep outside cornerman's direction, he must make sure it is a run and then attack the ball carrier from an outside-in angle, always squeezing the angle tighter as he approaches the ball carrier.

If a sprint-out pass comes his way, the outside cornerman is assigned to drop back and protect his outside deep one-third zone.

If the sprint-out pass goes away, the deep backside pass defender is taught to drop back into his deep one-third outside pass area. The farther the ball goes away, the closer the deep outside cornerman moves his zone area to the sprint-out quarterback. This continual sprint-out away action makes it a more difficult task for the passer to throw the throw-back pass into the deep backside, one-third zone.

The deep outside cornerman is assigned the deep outside one-third pass zone on all drop-back or pull-up pass plays.

Defensive Middle Safetyman: The deep middle safetyman is assigned to line head up on the center about eight to ten yards deep. The middle safetyman uses a parallel stance and keys the quarterback. As soon as the ball is put into play, the middle safetyman is taught to take a shuffle step backward. The middle safetyman must think "Pass" first and must never make the mistake of coming up too soon to make the tackle on a faking back. The middle safety is similar to a center fielder in baseball, and must be ready to sprint left or right to help out or back up either wide cornerman.

If a running play comes his way, he should attack the ball carrier head on; if a sweep develops, the middle safetyman is coached to attack the ball carrier, using an inside-out angle.

If the running play goes away, the middle safetyman must adjust his angle of pursuit so that he will be able to cut off the ball carrier. If a sprint-out pass develops in either direction, the quarterback is coached to defend his deep middle one-third, going deep as the deepest receiver.

When the passer drops straight back into a drop-back pass pattern, the deep middle safetyman is responsible to cover the deep middle one-third zone.

There are several other methods of pass defense used from the three-deep secondary alignment: man-to-man, rotation, leveling, and a combination of man-to-man and zone pass defense; but the three-deep, locked in, zone pass defense is the basic and simplest method of defending a pass whenever the defense employs an eight-man front defense.

STUNTING SECONDARY

A minimum amount of stunting is done in the Fifty-three Stack secondary, and then only in strategic locations on the football field. If we are using a three-deep secondary, we may stunt our outside safetyman and sprint him into the flat instead of his customary deep one-third zone assignment. This means that on occasion the outside deep cornerman may stunt out of his regular seven-yard deep alignment, shoot into the flat and bump the outside receiver off stride, and take the flat zone. The middle safetyman is then assigned to take the deep outside one-third zone, which is shortened in this case by the sidelines. The backside deep cornerman is now assigned to take the deep two-thirds zone in case of a pass. The backside linebacker is also called upon to cushion his area as he drops back on a sprint-out or play action pass away from his position.

The cushioning outside linebacker continues to drop or cushion backward until he is in a position as to help out the backside cornerman with his large two-thirds defensive pass zone responsibility (Diagram 9-15).

11

The Four-Deep Pass Defense

The Four-Deep Pass Defense is used primarily with the seven-man fronts of the Fifty Defenses. The exception to this rule is when these defenses employ the Monster Three-Deep Pass Defenses.

The Four-Deep Pass Defense is the best secondary defense to cover the wide varieties of offensive formation used in modern football. The Four-Deep secondary has many pass defense adjustments which may be used to cover the wide receivers. The man-to-man, revolving zones, invert, and level-off change ups, along with the combination of these calls, may continually confuse the offensive quarterback's passing strategy.

TWO-WAY PASS DEFENSE

The pass defense must incorporate two different attack patterns versus the offensive sprint-out, drop-back (pro), and bootleg passing attack. Utilizing these two methods of attacking the opponent's passing game keeps the offensive quarterback off guard and guessing versus our pass defense strategy. We also use a three, four, seven, or eight-man pass rush, because we always want to use a minimum rush and maximum number of pass defenders or a maximum rush and a minimum amount of pass defenders. Thus, our pass rush-coverage defense ratio is usually 3-8, 4-7, 8-3, or 7-4. We believe a more even 5-6 or 6-5 ratio does not accomplish either an effective pocket rush or an effective pass defense against a sound pass offense.

The Four-Deep Secondary accomplishes this coverage concept with its many different defensive coverage patterns.

Another advantage of the four-deep secondary is that the offensive motion is easily covered by the deep backs rather than by the linebackers. It is easier to adjust the deep men, just prior to the snap of the ball, versus motion because they are deeper and have a better view of the entire offensive formation than the linebackers. Since today's passers are throwing the ball more, there is no definite passing down; therefore, the four-deep secondary is the best deep alignment to disguise the pass coverage just prior to the snap of the ball. We like to use this Four-Deep Secondary with the Fifty and Pro Defense. We use the Four-Deep Man-to-Man Defense whenever we blitz off this defense.

FOUR-DEEP SECONDARY STANCE

The secondary defender should line up with his knees slightly bent, his weight on the balls of his feet, and his shoulders parallel to the line of scrimmage. The outside foot should be slightly back in a heel-toe relationship with the front foot. The defender should be in a two-point stance, bending at the waist with a parallel stance. His feet should be spread apart slightly less than his shoulders' width. His arms should hang freely down just inside his knees. His head should be up, with eyes focusing upon the defender's key.

ALIGNMENT

Cornermen usually line up three yards wide of any tight receivers. Never line up closer than six yards from the sidelines. The depth of the cornerman is five yards against tight formations and six, seven, or eight yards deep depending upon the width of the split or wide receiver. (See Split Rule.)

The safetyman lines up eight yards deep on the inside shoulder of the tight end against a tight formation. If a level call has been called to the safetyman's side, he will move deeper, from nine to ten yards deep, so he will be able to cover the deep outside one-third zone. The safetyman's depth is moved up, closer to the line of scrimmage, when we are in our goal line defense.

SPLIT RULE (ADJUSTMENT TO FLANKER OR SPLIT END)

1. Four- to seven-yard split—Line up on outside shoulder.

2. Seven- to ten-yard split—Line up on inside shoulder.
3. Ten or more yards split—Line up one yard inside the wide receiver.
4. Never line up closer than six yards from the sidelines.

OUTSIDE CUSHION

The secondary defender must continually be "outside conscious" because he always has help to the inside from one of his other three-deep defenders. He must maintain an outside-deep cushion on the potential receiver. This cushion is required so that the defender can watch the ball through the receiver. The secondary defender is always in a perfect position to attack the ball through the head of the receiver. A good cushion is assured by the deep defender, who always gets a good jump on the ball into his zone or good pre-pass position on the receiver in a man-to-man pass defense.

RUN RESPONSIBILITY

The defensive cornerman should attack the sweep, moving upfield, aiming at a point two yards outside the containing defender on or outside of the line of scrimmage. At times, it may be a linebacker or a defensive end. The cornerman should use a force-contain technique, that both forces the ball carrier inside the cornerman's position and contains the sweep. He should attack the sweep from an outside-in position. If the defender who is assigned to tackle the quarterback on an option play is unable to make the tackle, the cornerman must attack the quarterback.

The defensive safetyman should attack the sweep revolving through the original position of the cornerman's alignment. He should attack the sweep mentally outside but physically inside. This means he should attack the sweep on an angle, thinking the ball carrier will break outside the cornerman's contain assignment. When this happens, the safetyman must contain the sweep. Attacking the sweep physically inside means that if the cornerman contains the sweep and forces the ball carrier to cut the play up inside the defensive cornerman, the defensive safetyman should make the tackle from a slight outside-in angle.

DEFENDING THE CURL OR HOOK PASS

The deep secondary defender is coached to attack the hook pass after it has been thrown. If the defender anticipates a curl or hook pass and attacks before the ball has been put in the air, the passer may pump fake and hit the receiver deep on a curl or hook and go. The defender is taught to hit the receiver in the small of his back with his forehead and to search the defender from the bottom up. The bottom-up search method is a technique where the defender shoots his arms up and under the receiver's arms and then pulls the receiver's arms down. The defender must be continually coached never to attack the hook pass until the ball is in the air.

As the secondary back approaches the curling or hooking potential receiver, he hollers "Hook, hook!" or "Curl, curl!" to alert the linebacker of the pass pattern the potential receiver is running. The linebacker needs help as he is sprinting to his drop zone watching the passer, and the potential receiver is behind him. A pattern call by the secondary defender helps to put the linebacker in the proper place to make the interception. Defensive pass communication is a prerequisite for a successful pass defense program.

SINGLE COVERAGE LEFT VS. TIGHT FORMATION (Diagram 11-1)

Left Cornerman

Stance: See stance.

Alignment: Three yards wide, outside the tight end's original position and five yards deep.

Run Responsibility—Action To: Attack the sweep, maintaining a two-yard outside relationship with the containing defender on or near the line of scrimmage.

Run Responsibility—Action Away: Check for reverse or counter action, and then sprint back to the deep outside one-third zone and get into the revolving pattern by revolving through the position of the near safetyman.

Pass Responsibility:

Sprint To: Revolve to the flat area and continue to drop back deep if no one shows in the flat zone.

Drop Back: If single call (left), take the flat zone area. If single call (right), drop back into deep outside one-third zone.

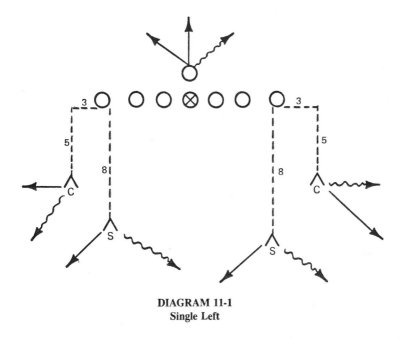

DIAGRAM 11-1
Single Left

Sprint Away: Drop back to the deep one-third zone to same side.

Left Safetyman

Stance: See stance.

Alignment: Line up eight yards deep on the inside shoulder of the tight end's original position. If wing or slot to that side, move to an outside shoulder position on the tight end.

Run Responsibility—Action To: Support by coming up outside the cornerman in a secondary support route.

Run Responsibility—Action Away: Sprint into revolve pattern after checking for a reverse or counter play. Revolve through the safetyman's position.

Pass Responsibility:

Sprint To: Defend the deep outside one-third zone.

Drop Back: Sprint to defend the deep middle one-third zone if call is away (right), and cover the deep outside one-third zone if the call is to left.

Sprint Away: Cover the deep middle one-third zone.

Right Safetyman

Stance: See stance.

Alignment: Line up eight yards deep on the inside shoulder of the tight end's original position. If wing or slot to that side, move to an outside shoulder position on the tight end.

Run Responsibility—Action To: Attack the sweep, maintaining a two-yard outside relationship with the containing defender on or near the line of scrimmage.

Run Responsibility—Action Away: Check for the reverse or counter action and then sprint to the deep outside one-third zone and get into the revolving pattern by revolving through the position of the near safetyman.

Pass Responsibility:

Sprint To: Defend the deep outside one-third zone.
Drop Back: If single call (left), defend the deep middle one-third zone. If single call (right), defend the deep outside one-third zone.
Sprint Away: Cover the deep middle one-third zone.

Right Cornerman

Stance: See stance.

Alignment: Three yards wide, outside the tight end's original position and five yards deep.

Run Responsibility—Action To: Attack the sweep, maintaining a two-yard outside relationship with the containing defender on or off the line of scrimmage.

Run Responsibility—Action Away: Check for the reverse or counter action and then sprint back to the deep outside one-third zone and get into the revolve pattern by revolving through the position of the near safetyman.

Pass Responsibility:

Sprint To: Revolve to the flat area and continue to drop back deep if no one shows in the flat zone.

Drop Back: If single call (right), take the flat zone area. If single call (left), take the deep one-third area to the same side.

Sprint Away: Drop back to the deep outside one-third zone to the same side.

Coaching Note: The single coverage call is used exclusively against the tight offensive formations. Once the offense begins to widen their offensive (a wide receiver to both sides), we will revolve using the Cover #1 call. (See Chapter 10 on Three-Deep Pass Defense Cover #1 Call.) We may stay in our four across the board by using our Change and Level Calls. (Check Change and Level Calls in this chapter.)

CHANGE COVERAGE (Diagram 11-2)

Corner to Side of Change Call

Stance: See stance.

Alignment: Tight formation to Call side—Line up three yards outside of tight end's original position and five yards deep.

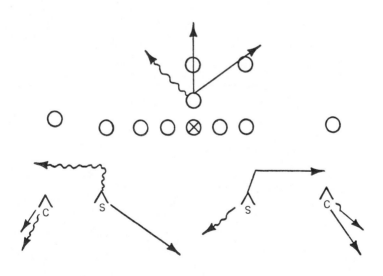

DIAGRAM 11-2
Change Coverage

Wide Formation to Call side—Use Split Rule:
Four- to seven-yard split—Six yards deep; outside shoulder.
Seven- to ten-yard split—Seven yards deep; inside shoulder.
Ten yards plus split—Eight yards deep; one yard inside.

Run Responsibility—Action To: First two-step shuffle to deep one-third outside zone, then make sure it is a sweep and attack as secondary contain man.

Run Responsibility—Action Away (Tight Formation): Take two-step shuffle to deep one-third outside zone, and then get into revolve pattern by revolving through the position of the near safetyman.

Pass Responsibility:

Action to: Deep outside one-third zone.
Drop Back: Deep outside one-third zone.
Action Away: Deep outside one-third zone.

Safety to Side of Change

Stance: See stance.

Alignment: Eight yards deep nose up on the tight end or the tight end's original position.

Run Responsibility—Action To: If the ball comes, start for flat area, then direct route for two-yard outside position of the end man on the line of scrimmage. Force contain the sweep.

Run Responsibility—Action Away: Sprint to the deep middle and continue revolving to the ball carrier.

Pass Responsibility:

Sprint To: Sprint to flat.
Drop Back: Sprint to flat.
Sprint Away: Sprint to deep middle one-third zone.

Safety Away from Change Call

Stance: See stance.

Alignment: Same as Single Coverage.

Run Responsibility To: Same as Single Coverage.

Run Responsibility Away: Same as Single Coverage.

Pass Responsibility:

Sprint To: Same as Single Coverage.
Drop Back: Same as Single Coverage.
Sprint Away: Same as Single Coverage.

Corner Away from Change Call

Stance: See stance.

Alignment: Same as Single Coverage.

Run Responsibility To: Same as Single Coverage.

Run Responsibility Away: Same as Single Coverage.

Pass Responsibility:

Sprint To: Same as Single Coverage.
Drop Back: Same as Single Coverage.
Sprint Away: Same as Single Coverage.

LEVEL COVERAGE (Diagram 11-3)

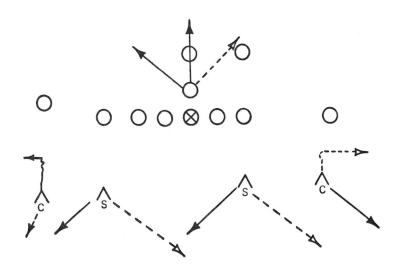

DIAGRAM 11-3
Level Coverage

Corner to Side of Level Call

Stance: See stance.

Alignment: Tight formation to Call side—Line up three yards outside of the tight end's original position and five yards deep.
Wide Formation to the Call side—Use Split Rule:
Four- to seven-yard split—Six yards deep; outside shoulder.
Seven- to ten-yard split—Seven yards deep; inside shoulder.
Ten yards plus split—Eight yards deep; one yard inside.

Run Responsibility—Action To: Hang and take one step up and chug the potential receiver if call is to your side or the ball comes your way. Then, level off and take the flat zone about seven yards deep. Attack the sweep by using a force-contain technique.

Run Responsibility—Action Away: Take two-step shuffle to the deep outside one-third outside zone and then get into the revolve pattern and cut off the ball carrier.

Pass Responsibility:

Sprint To: Chug potential wide receiver, and then level off and defend the flat zone.
Drop Back: Chug potential wide receiver and then level off and defend the flat zone.
Sprint Away: Defend deep outside one-third zone.

Safety to Side of the Level Call

Stance: See stance.

Alignment: Nine to ten yards deep, nose up on the tight end or tight end's original position.

Run Responsibility—Action To: On the sweep, attack the outside as the secondary contain man.

Run Responsibility—Action Away: Sprint to the deep middle and continue revolving to the ball carrier.

Pass Responsibility:

Sprint To: Deep outside one-third zone.
Drop Back: Deep outside one-third zone.
Sprint Away: Deep middle one-third zone.

Safety Away from the Level Call

Stance: See stance.

Alignment: Same as Single Call.

Run Responsibility To: Same as Single Call.

Run Responsibility Away: Same as Single Call.

Pass Responsibility:

Sprint To: Same as Single Call.
Drop Back: Same as Single Call.
Sprint Away: Same as Single Call.

Corner Away from Level Call

Stance: See stance.

Alignment: Same as Single Call.

Run Responsibility To: Same as Single Call.

Run Responsibility Away: Same as Single Call.

Pass Responsibility:

Sprint To: Same as Single Call.
Drop Back: Same as Single Call.
Sprint Away: Same as Single Call.

SINGLE X COVERAGE LEFT

Same as Cover #1 in Chapter 10 on Three-Deep Pass Coverage.

Coaching Note: Rover-Linebacker would be the left safetyman in Single X Coverage Left.

DOUBLE X COVERAGE LEFT VS. WIDE FORMATION
(Diagram 11-4)

Left Corner

Stance: See stance.

Alignment: Use Split Rule.

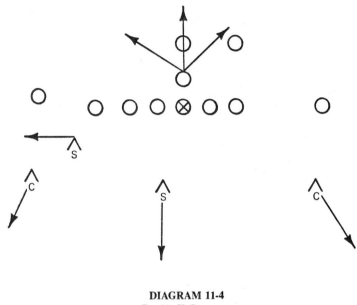

DIAGRAM 11-4
Double X Coverage

Run Responsibility—Action To: Shuffle back to deep outside one-third zone; then attack sweep as secondary contain man.

Run Responsibility—Action Away: Shuffle back to deep outside one-third zone, take a picture, then get into revolve pattern and take a course to cut off the ball carrier.

Pass Responsibility:

Sprint To: Deep outside one-third zone. Locked in all the way.
Drop Back: Deep outside one-third zone. Locked in all the way.
Sprint Away: Deep outside one-third zone. Locked in all the way.

Left Safety

Stance: See stance.

Alignment: Use walk-away position three yards deep, and split the difference between the wide receiver and the next eligible receiver.

Run Responsibility—Action To: Force contain the sweep.

Run Responsibility—Action Away: Sprint to the deep middle one-third zone and then get into the revolve pattern to cut off the ball carrier.

Pass Responsibility:

Sprint To: Cover flat. Locked in all the way.
Drop Back: Cover flat. Locked in all the way.
Sprint Away: Cover flat. Locked in all the way.

Right Safety

Stance: See stance.

Alignment: Line up ten yards deep, approximately head up on the offensive center.

Run Responsibility—Action To: Revolve toward the sweep and attack the ball carrier, using an inside-out angle.

Run Responsibility—Action Away: Revolve toward the sweep and attack the ball carrier, using an inside-out angle.

Pass Responsibility:

Sprint To: Cover deep middle one-third. Locked in all the way.
Drop Back: Cover deep middle one-third. Locked in all the way.
Sprint Away: Cover deep middle one-third. Locked in all the way.

Right Corner

Stance: See stance.

Alignment: Tight formation—Three yards wide and five yards deep. Wide formation—Use Split Rule.

Run Responsibility—Action To: Attack the sweep, maintaining a two-yard outside relationship with the defender on or near the line of scrimmage. Force contain the sweep and make the tackle.

Run Responsibility—Action Away: Shuffle back to the deep one-third zone and then revolve to cut off the ball carrier.

Pass Responsibility:

Sprint To: Cover deep outside one-third. Locked in all the way.
Drop Back: Cover deep outside one-third. Locked in all the way.
Sprint Away: Cover deep outside one-third. Locked in all the way.

MAN-TO-MAN COVERAGE (FOUR DEEP) (Diagram 11-5)

Left and Right Corners

Stance: See stance.

Alignment: Tight Formation—Two yards wide and six yards deep. Wide Formation—Use Split Rule.

Run Responsibility—Action To: Attack the sweep, maintaining a two-yard outside relationship with the end man on the line of scrimmage. Contain the sweep.

Run Responsibility—Action Away: Check man and then get into proper revolve pattern, revolving through the near safetyman's position.

Pass Responsibility—Tight Formation: Use the Inside-Outside pass coverage to your side:

1. Both receivers cross—Take outside man.
2. Both receivers outside—Take shortest man.
3. Both receivers inside—Take the shortest man.
4. Only one receiver out—Take him.

Pass Responsibility—Wide Formation Your Side: Cover the widest eligible potential receiver man to man.

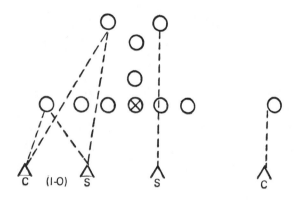

DIAGRAM 11-5
Man-to-Man Coverage

Left and Right Safety

Stance: See stance.

Alignment: Seven yards deep, lining up on the inside shoulder of the tight end; and, when there are two wide receivers, play on the inside shoulder of the inside receiver.

Run Responsibility—Action To: Support by coming up outside the cornerman's position if the offense is tight. Contain the sweep in an invert type of technique if the offensive formation has a wide receiver to your side.

Run Responsibility—Action Away: Check for counters and reverses and then get into the revolving pattern to head off the ball carrier.

Pass Responsibility—Tight Formation: Use the Inside-Outside pass coverage to your side:

1. Both receivers cross—Take the inside man.
2. Both receivers outside—Take the deepest man.
3. Both receivers inside—Take the deepest man.
4. Only one receiver out—You are free safety.

Pass Responsibility—Wide Formation Your Side: Cover key, man to man. If he blocks, you are free safety; unless instructed differently, go to the deep middle one-third zone.

FOUR-DEEP VERSUS MOTION

Man-to-Man to Zone: If Cover Four (Man-to-Man) has been called and there is long motion to the strength of the formation, the defensive secondary signal caller calls the direction of the motion (left) and calls Level (left). This motion call takes us out of our Four Call (Man-to-Man) and puts us into a Level (Zone) call to the side of the strength of the formation (Diagram 11-6). The left corner is assigned to chug the potential wide receiver so that the left safetyman has time to cover the deep outside left one-third zone. The backside (right) safetyman revolves to the deep middle zone and the backside (right) corner takes the deep outside one-third zone away from motion. We move to a zone call because the motion has caused the formation to go unbalanced to the side of the two

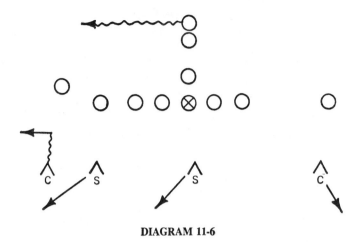

DIAGRAM 11-6

wide backs. Regardless of how many receivers the offense sends out to the zone side, we feel the zone defense can handle all of these receivers because the secondary defenders are only covering an area or zone.

Man-to-Man All the Way (Diagram 11-7)—If man-to-man (Cover Four) has been called and motion is away from the strength of the formation, resulting in a double wing or balanced formation, the secondary call remains Cover Four or man-to-man. The man who has the motion man slides along the line in front of the right cornerback and takes the motion

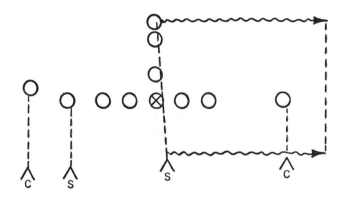

DIAGRAM 11-7

man all the way man to man. All of the other secondary defenders play their men man to man (Diagram 11-7).

If the offense uses a great many picking defenders, the defensive secondary may use a bump technique whereby the right safetyman moves over and picks up the offensive left tight end man to man and "bumps" the right cornerback to pick up the long motion man in a Cover Four (man-to-man) assignment. The left corner and safetyman play their assigned receivers man to man all the way (Diagram 11-8).

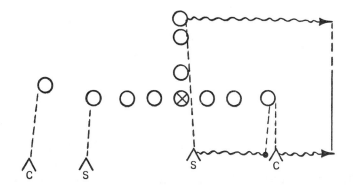

DIAGRAM 11-8

Coaching Note: The left safety must remind the linebacker that he has the fullback in a man-to-man assignment if the fullback releases for a pass. This is especially true versus a Pro formation and split backs. The linebacker must key the remaining back man to man all the way.

Zone to Man (Diagram 11-9)—If a zone call (Double X Left) has been made, we will stay in that zone call if motion goes toward the strength of the formation. When motion goes away from the formation, resulting in a double wing or balanced formation, the defensive secondary signal caller is taught to call Cover Four (man-to-man). Cover Four calls for the right safetyman to move in the direction of the motion and picks up the tight end man to man. He bumps the cornerman who is then assigned to cover the widest receiver, the long motion man. The Up Safetyman moves from his three-yard deep walk-away position and picks up the offensive right tight end man to man. The left defensive cornerman is isolated on the flanker man to man.

The change over from zone to man-to-man is brought about

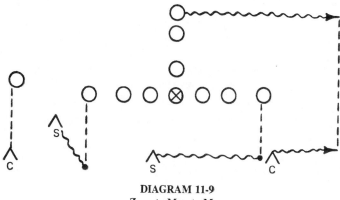

DIAGRAM 11-9
Zone to Man-to-Man

smoothly by continually practicing this technique in daily practice sessions. We teach our defensive secondary defenders that they must always check their potential man-to-man assignments whenever a zone call has been made, because motion may put them into a man-to-man assignment.

MAN-TO-MAN COVERAGE VS. WIDE RECEIVER (Diagram 11-10)

The first pass the man-to-man defender must stop is the post (down, in and deep) pass pattern. Therefore, to defend successfully against this pass pattern, the defender is coached to line up on the potential receiver's inside shoulder. This alignment forces the potential pass receiver to run over the defender if he attempts the post pattern.

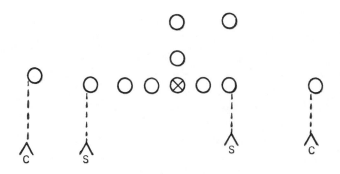

DIAGRAM 11-10
Man-To-Man Coverage

The defender must be taught to sprint to the outside and go through the receiver's outside shoulder whenever the receiver attempts to break to the outside. If the potential receiver attempts to run a go or straight up deep pattern, the defender must sprint deep and get into the receiver's ear.

Another method used by the deep outside secondary man is to align on the outside shoulder of the potential pass defender and force the receiver to cut to the inside. This outside technique is good for a couple of reasons: it may take away the receiver's favorite outside pass pattern; it forces the receiver into the free safetyman's area; and it may also give the outside pass defender a chance to chug or bump the wide receiver to throw off his pass pattern timing.

Therefore, we teach our cornerman or wide defender to use the outside alignment when he has a free safetyman to his inside, and to use an inside alignment whenever the defender does not have a free safetyman to his inside.

MIDDLE LINEBACKER'S PASS DEFENSE (ZONE) (Diagram 11-11)

Against a pro-break passing formation, we coach the middle linebacker (Pro Fifty-three) to key the strong side running back. This key helps to minimize the threat of the offensive flare control passing attack (Diagram 11-11). If the strong side running back blocks (Diagram 11-11),

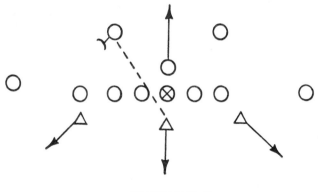

DIAGRAM 11-11

the middle linebacker is taught to drop straight back into the middle hook zone. If the strong side running back swings toward the tight end side and the quarterback drops straight back for a pass, the middle linebacker is

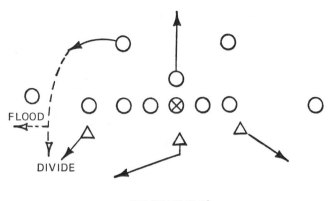

DIAGRAM 11-12

coached to drop back in a 45 degree angle toward the direction of the swinging back and look for a flood or a divide pass pattern (Diagram 11-12). If the strong side offensive running back sprints toward the split end's side, the middle linebacker drops back on a 45 degree angle toward the split end side and looks for a possible flood pass pattern to the split end's side (Diagram 11-13).

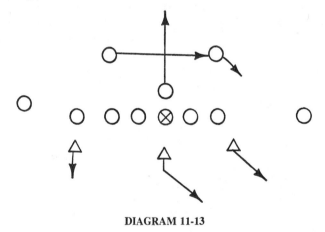

DIAGRAM 11-13

Against the sprint-out pass, the middle linebacker is taught to sprint to the hook zone in the direction of the sprint out. If no receiver is in the hook zone, the middle linebacker is coached to continue on to the curl zone. If the strong side linebacker is in the pass coverage, the middle linebacker is assigned second contain responsibilities (Diagram 11-14).

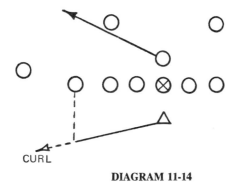

DIAGRAM 11-14

MIDDLE LINEBACKER'S PASS DEFENSE (MAN-TO-MAN)
(Diagram 11-15)

If the pro-break formation's strong side running back is a threat on running divide and flood pass patterns, the middle linebacker may be forced to move his alignment over to the strong side of the offensive formation. This would also involve moving the defensive strong side tackle closer to the center, to take on added middle responsibilities versus the offensive middle running attack. This move would then place the middle linebacker on a man-to-man assignment on the strong side running back (Diagram 11-15). This would give the defense a free safetyman and would also allow the strong side linebacker a chance to blitz or play normal.

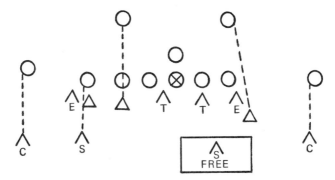

DIAGRAM 11-15
Middle Linebacker M/M

If the opposition attempted to pick off the middle linebacker with the tight end and run the strong side running back on a flat or divide pass pattern (Diagram 11-16), we would have to make a linebacker adjustment.

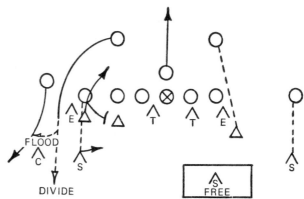

DIAGRAM 11-16

The defensive adjustment would be an inside "Banjo Call." This would place the middle linebacker and the outside linebacker on an inside-outside defensive pass assignment. This means that the middle linebacker and the strong side linebacker would both key the strong side running back and the tight end. The strong side linebacker would pick up the strong side running back if he ran an outside route (Diagram 11-17). If the tight end also ran outside, the strong side linebacker would take the widest receiver (Diagram 11-18). If only the tight end ran outside, the strong side linebacker would play the tight end (Diagram 11-19). The middle linebacker would play the tight end if he broke inside, and the outside linebacker would play the strong side running back if he broke

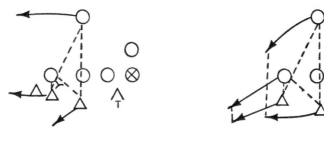

DIAGRAM 11-17   **DIAGRAM 11-18**

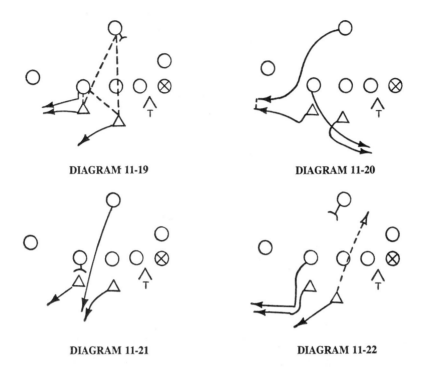

DIAGRAM 11-19

DIAGRAM 11-20

DIAGRAM 11-21

DIAGRAM 11-22

outside (Diagram 11-20). If the tight end blocked and the strong side running back broke inside, the middle linebacker would play him man to man (Diagram 11-21). If the running back blocked and the tight end ran a flat pass pattern, the strong side linebacker would take the tight end man to man, and the middle linebacker would be free to drop to the hook zone or blitz the passer, depending upon the pregame defensive strategy (Diagram 11-22).

The "Banjo Call" would fire up the strong side safetyman so the defense would now have two deep free safetymen (Diagram 11-23).

If we still want only the weakside safetyman free, we teach our outside strong linebacker and middle linebacker to play inside-outside on the strong side running back only. Therefore, if the strong side running back swings wide, the strong side linebacker plays him man to man (Diagram 11-24). If the running back breaks through the line inside the offensive end's original position, the middle linebacker plays the potential pass receiver man to man (Diagram 11-25). A predetermined blitz assignment may be given to the linebacker who is not assigned to play the

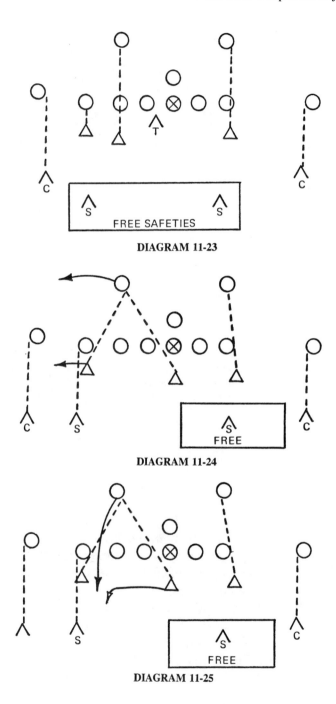

DIAGRAM 11-23

DIAGRAM 11-24

DIAGRAM 11-25

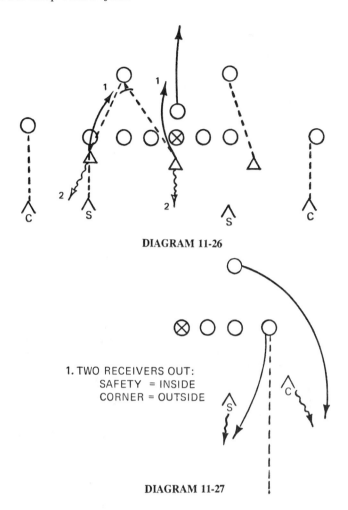

DIAGRAM 11-26

1. TWO RECEIVERS OUT:
   SAFETY = INSIDE
   CORNER = OUTSIDE

DIAGRAM 11-27

strong side running back man to man. If the running back blocks, to protect the passer, both linebackers are free to blitz or both of them may be assigned to play their normal hook areas. This gives the secondary defense one free safetyman and places the strong side safetyman man to man on the tight end (Diagram 11-26).

With two close offensive receivers (*example*: tight end-wingback), our two deep pass defenders play a "Combo Call." "Combo" stands for cornerback and safetyman to play inside-outside coverage similar to the linebacker's "Banjo Call" previously discussed.

Diagram 11-27 illustrates a veer back being covered by the cornerback and the safetyman picking up the inside cutting tight end. This is Inside (Safety)—Outside (Corner) Coverage.

In Diagram 11-28, both receivers break inside; safety takes shortest and cornerback takes deepest receiver.

If the wingback breaks into the outside flat, the cornerman takes him, while the safetyman picks up the tight end on a flag cut. Both receivers outside cuts—safety-deepest, corner-shortest (Diagram 11-29).

When the set halfback blocks and the ball comes, the safety takes the one receiver and the cornerback is the free secondary defender (Diagram 11-30).

If the ball goes away and the one remaining back (slot man) blocks, now the corner is responsible to play the remaining receiver man to man and the safetyman is free (Diagram 11-31).

The reader should study Diagrams 11-27 through 11-31 because they have not only a clear visual illustration, but they also have a written guide to help the reader understand the complete "Combo Call" concept.

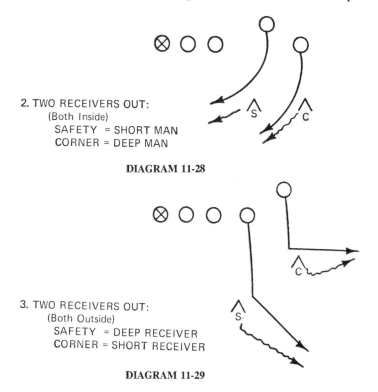

2. TWO RECEIVERS OUT:
(Both Inside)
SAFETY = SHORT MAN
CORNER = DEEP MAN

DIAGRAM 11-28

3. TWO RECEIVERS OUT:
(Both Outside)
SAFETY = DEEP RECEIVER
CORNER = SHORT RECEIVER

DIAGRAM 11-29

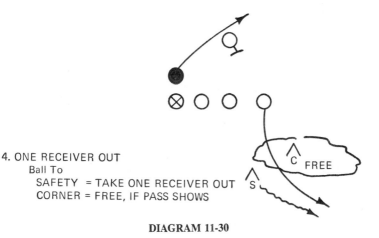

4. ONE RECEIVER OUT
   Ball To
       SAFETY = TAKE ONE RECEIVER OUT
       CORNER = FREE, IF PASS SHOWS

DIAGRAM 11-30

5. ONE RECEIVER OUT
   (Ball Away)
       SAFETY = REVOLVE & FREE
       CORNER = TAKE ONE RECEIVER OUT

DIAGRAM 11-31

Index